The Bower

Thirty-Five Years of
PHOENIX POETS

CONNIE VOISINE

The Bower

THE UNIVERSITY OF CHICAGO PRESS

Chicago and London

The University of Chicago Press, Chicago 60637
The University of Chicago Press, Ltd., London
© 2019 by The University of Chicago
All rights reserved. No part of this book may be used or reproduced
in any manner whatsoever without written permission, except in
the case of brief quotations in critical articles and reviews. For more
information, contact the University of Chicago Press, 1427 East 60th
Street, Chicago, IL 60637.
Published 2019
Printed in the United States of America

28 27 26 25 24 23 22 21 20 19   1 2 3 4 5

ISBN-13: 978-0-226-61378-9 (paper)
ISBN-13: 978-0-226-61381-9 (e-book)
DOI: https://doi.org/10.7208/chicago/9780226613819.001.0001

Library of Congress Cataloging-in-Publication Data

Names: Voisine, Connie, author.
Title: The bower / Connie Voisine.
Other titles: Phoenix poets.
Description: Chicago ; London : The University of Chicago Press, 2019. |
    Series: Phoenix poets
Identifiers: LCCN 2018035073 | ISBN 9780226613789 (pbk. : alk. paper) |
    ISBN 9780226613819 (ebook)
Classification: LCC PS3622.O37 B69 2019 | DDC 811/.6—dc23
LC record available at https://lccn.loc.gov/2018035073

♾ This paper meets the requirements of ANSI/NISO Z39.48-1992
(Permanence of Paper).

I will build my love a bower
Near yon pure crystal fountain
And on it I will pile
All the flowers of the mountain

Wild Mountain Thyme, traditional folk ballad

ACKNOWLEDGMENTS

The author would like to thank the editors of the following magazines for printing the following poems, or versions thereof, sometimes under different titles:

Ambit no. 230 (2017): selections from *The Bower*
Ilanot Review (Winter 2018): selections from *The Bower*
Plume Anthology of Poetry 4 (2016): "Easy for Me"
Tinderbox 2, no. 6 (April 2016): "A root of bane" as "Touch Me Not"

There are many in Belfast who made us feel welcome and without whose generosity so much would have been much less. Thanks to the Ormeau Road crew: Eilish and Bernie Stocks; Dave and Kerry Cullen and their children, Eve, Molly, Nell, and Fin; Hazlett Keers and Kate McBrien; and the Ormeau Road Boxing Club. The writers who lunched: Frank Ormsby, Malachi O'Doherty, and Maureen Boyle. The welcoming Fergus Woods and Mary Durkin. The Fulbright organization, Queen's University (Dr. Brian Caraher, who greeted us well), and the people who first went with us there: Jeffrey and Jennifer Thompson and family, Scott and Mary Bell Boltwood and family, Zev Trachtenberg and Tina Kambour and family. The Fulbrighters since: Erika Meitner, Tess Taylor, James Arthur, and Meg Tyler. Botanic Primary School, the wee school that gave our child friendship and an excellent education. Thanks for the good work of Katy Radford and Neil Jarman and family. The traditional music community that opened its doors: Martin and Christine Dowling, Melanie Houton, Connor Caldwell,

Stevie Porter, Brendan O'Hare, Friday evenings at the Rose and Crown, and Síle Boylan and Gerry O'Connor and family. Oh, and more writers: Emma Must, Kathleen McCracken, Jan Carson, Leontia Flynn, Stephen Sexton, Stephen Connolly and Manuela Moser, Shelley Tracey, and Carrie Etter (across the North Sea via Illinois). John T. Davis, his love for Belfast and our Western desert. Thanks to No Alibis Bookstore—and David Torrans and Claudia Edelmann—you are the first place we go.

And thanks to the Yanks who love and keep me here, writers and friends: Sheila Black, Jennifer Bartlett, Marianne Boruch, Robert Boswell, Karen Brennan, Richard Greenfield, Dana and Juniper Kroos, Antonya Nelson, Jacqueline Osherow, and the writers of Warren Wilson.

More than everything to my dearests, Rus and Alma.

The Bower

The summer before we packed for Belfast, my daughter D
grew committed to butterflies, crossing streets at a flash

of color, crouching in the grass by peonies with hands
cupped, still until she pounced. D, the terrible queen

of insects. Fireflies were cake work, ladybugs too random.
She argued with me, *I will not touch their wings.* Impossible,

though I pretended otherwise. For weeks she'd been working
on a moving panorama, a scroll depicting a Scottish ballad

about a lover who builds a bower of *wild mountain thyme
all around the blooming heather,* and she sang for me

without shyness its refrain, *Will ye go, lassie, go?*
as we walked together. But a bloodied shirt was stuck

to tar at the end of the alley, and a tall, Kevlared cop
pointed her manicured finger toward the trash cans,

a stack of abandoned suitcases. Maybe we should not
have watched as the busy ones set up police tape

from one side of the street to the other, as a woman
sat on the curb with her head in her hands, shiny curls

separating in her grip, a sweatshirt bound about
her pregnant belly. "Panorama" comes from the Greek

"to see" and "all." In the nineteenth century it was a popular
form of entertainment, the painted scroll cranked

through images and stories while a narrator called
the Delineator recited, sang and stirred feelings.

That afternoon a darkness punctured the silken sun,
the slippery ordinary, a knife still in the hand of someone

young and unknown who stood fearless, his face
made of a bright, new material. Two others received

wounds—arms, torso—and maybe it humiliated,
our watching them step into the ambulance,

the two made obedient by their survival.
We had been on our way, our particular

zigzag of shortcuts, pretty trees, quieter blocks,
rogue irises, and rattraps from the government, boxes

set here and there printed with DO NOT TAMPER.
There was the dog certain in his grizzled blindness

and habit barking right up to a fence long since gone.
Thick antennae unfurled from a TV station van

and so the day entered neighborhood fame,
the neighbor Maria into the proffered microphone,

Twenty-seven years and never have I. My daughter
asked, *What is isolated incident?* The ballad much later

finishes, *If my true love she were gone, I would surely
find another*, which makes me laugh. The replaceable

beloved, the next true one for whom the fragrant bower
always waits beside a crystal fountain. D says,

You got it wrong, Mama. She knows I built the bower
for her and all the butterflies she will capture.

*

Pieces of the day: the fraternal order's parade of children
in small suits with epaulets, banners, and drums. My husband,

H, requests a photograph and is met with a smile. I'm confused
at their martial joy but D is not. She wants it all: drum, flag,

regalia galore. An image of the grave containing the three
famous Irish saints above a cash register. Stacked newspapers

feature a man carrying a child, kicked as he runs for a border
in some other European country. The gray cat lolling on the sunny
    stones

bears a collar: LADY. *That wee'un, always in the streets*,
says a neighbor. David's hallucinations from the Parkinson's

drugs, the specter at the periphery, *Do you know the way
a coat looks, hung on the back of the door at night?*

That's who they are. A man sleeping it off half on, half off
the pavement moaning to police and social worker,

I am wrecked. I think it's urine in the bottle he clutches.
D scratches Lady while I describe "fair-weather friend"

for how the gray cat hides on rainy days. This is the gift:
a year without work at half pay and a life far enough away.

My kin never got paid for nothing or something like poems.
Admire the cook outside the chipper smoking cigarettes at the curb,

his clothes still immaculately white. Workers in cherry pickers
remove lamppost flags left after parading season, months

late (Commission rules) above this ragged display, a toddler parade
in peacetime. All I've done with my own life is change

my social class invisibly, alone. Somali girls, refugees,
down the street lounge on their trampoline (D says, *Lucky!*)

in their middle-blue Holy Rosary Primary School jumpers,
    dreaming
on slow clouds, gray skies, the same fat gulls spiraling through.

*

In the books I've read and talks I've heard, the conflict
scholars say "pornography of violence," or "new kinds of memories,"

and nineteen years into the staggering notion of peace
is forgetting still perhaps the best option? I have found

so many ugly stories—a woman raped in a bed beside
her murdered son, Remembrance Day celebrations bombed,

three generations in one family gone. Does a person need
more stories? Colin Davidson paints the portraits of survivors;

the show is up in the small, well-used Ulster Museum.
Known for celebrity portraits, he paints the faces,

shoulders, a glimpse of shirt of a Brad Pitt or a Heaney
and now these unknown. No smiles, paint thick to make

bone and light of colors that are mostly dull,
hair floating into backgrounds of unintelligible places.

These eyes are precise, though, so finely made. Eighteen portraits
of those stove in by loss. The labels identify the bereaved.

I learn who was killed and the barest details of how.
Some are survivors of violence themselves and I read acid,

car, gun. Hard to tell why or what side are they if any,
who and what affiliation the killers. An interpreter

tells me a victim's group made introductions to the painter
and none are for sale, that she will refer those who request it

to trauma care or Victims Services. My daughter takes
the survey upon leaving. I write for her, *It might help*

to have sounds and things you can touch. What kinds of things?
I don't know, her hair, some clothes, the bomb?

At the Victorian B and B in Derry the woman lets her bulldog,
Bertie, lather D's face. Her husband is away in Panama

researching the Scots province of Darien. *The one Keats
mentions in "On First Looking into Chapman's Homer,"*

my husband points out. *Well, sure*, she says. The story is
a group of Scots left their home on boats—*Saint Andrew,*

Caledonia, Unicorn, Dolphin, and *Endeavour*—signed treaties
with native peoples to begin again in New Caledonia.

They foundered under pressure from Spaniards, diseases,
costing Scotland a quarter of its wealth at the time.

What hubris (old nag) blinded them to the difficulties
of empire? I say, smartass, *They had no slaves nor*

could they make some. Keats loves the colonizer's
wild surmise: Cortez, who never was there on Darien Peak,

surveys the prospect with eagle eyes. The world's oceans,
turns out, met only in Keats's eye, Keats who doesn't mention

the folly of the Scots, but why would he? Everyone knew
the grim bits: failed finances, disease, men in wools

paying for work with booze. Derry is said to be the last,
the only walled city left in Ireland, and we can see that wall

from our room. From turret to black cannon we run along
its wide, avenued top. *What if it snowed and I had a sled?*

D wants to know as we gaze down one sloping view,
complete with hillocks and curves. Ah, a clean, white path.

At a few corners the top widens for restored cannons, one
"Roaring Meg," which in 1689 protected Protestants from Catholics

attacking the walls. Kids love a cannon—the wood wheel
is a ladder, scoot up, or slide down the barrel. Atop one might see

over the wall to a mural of a schoolgirl killed in recent wars,
the words D can't yet care about (how could I make it so

she never needed to?) or words reminding Catholics
to stay out. This world waits, inscribed in ways not always

as clear: Bertie's a bulldog because of who his owners are.
Bertie's name is that of an English king—the son

of Queen Victoria, the "uncle" of Europe. He licks my hands.
That night the Traveler piper plays wildly on a small stage

flanked by fiddlers from England, Scotland, and Oregon.
He quits midtune to tell the guitarist to stop his strum.

I can't hear myself in all this, he growls, begins again, alone.

*

The gift to our girl is a book of Irish legends. We settle in
to read them. The dark started earlier today and

haunted our walk home from school, over Kings Bridge
and the River Lagan. Our herons were lost in the murk

but we saw the rower inside her lit skull, an arrow
through the dusk. *Once upon a time, a girl named Fionnuala,*

I start. D's buried in soft animal toys, duvet, and pillows,
She was as beautiful as sunshine on blossomed branches.

Once upon a time, St. Stephen's Day in Knocknagree,
"the hill of the hare," I sat and drank in a packed room

lit by fire, before my girl was born. A singer stood as if centuries
had not passed. O his song, how it broke all hearts that night.

A song of baroque custom, of ornamented, winged trill,
and O the lean rise of his lament, curving facade of sound

then hiss of sibilant. O broken umbrella between the wind and
my wind-chapped cheeks. *This is the land of song.* I felt it.

Of lush, maximalist Song. *Her brother Aodh was like a young eagle
in the blue of the sky; and her others, Fiacra and Conn,*

were as beautiful as running water. Before drifting off
D performs the tasks for safe passage—kiss the bear, flip the pillow,

turn on the night-light teacher gave for being good—then asks me,
When did this story happen? The books say it's one of the three

great tragedy narratives from before St. Patrick and in those days sorrow was not known in Ireland. I tell her, *Before everything.*

*

I use money like a stranger, an immigrant, break large
bills because I cannot recognize the coins fast enough

in line at the shops. I hold out a fistful and ask whomever
to take the price. The weighty coins clank in my purse,

my trouser pockets, my coat. I wander like Marley's ghost,
managing my various regrets, vanities, fears to a clink,

clink, clink. To the butcher, the baker, and all the way home.
Today I feel dully mad and unreasonably dulled by

repetition. I come home and drop by drop the leak
has filled the sink completely with a waste of water.

Once I had friends who laughed in bed. I heard them
through the walls. I once had a friend who slept in her uniform,

a synthetic tux, to save time for the morning commute
to Radio City Music Hall. Once I had a friend who was me and

I had a friend once a long time ago. It was not so long ago
(you see, Marley?), but maybe I was always this way—

do I recall any other? Soundproof the walls and keep walking.
Watching a zombie serial I mute the battle scenes as innocents

are consumed alongside the guilty in snarling, splashing
waves of flesh. I prefer the program's moral questions—

Are the dead able to hate? Is it murder when they eat you?
Shouldn't the living try to get along to better scavenge, fight?

And why do the living fight at all? For our memories
of the lives we had, for what we squander?

*

I'm back at the museum where people enter free of charge
due to government gift, and during these thick, rainy days

it's hard not to. A painting of the 12th of July, a day for marchers,
for the losers who still suffer loss in burning piles of trash

with holy men hung in effigy, bloody songs sung by some
about the others, some drunk, some unemployed, some

who consider it their identity. The painting is controversial,
the marchers depicted in white hoods, KKK-like, here

at the public museum. What would Rembrandt say? His face
glows a honey gold, a self-portrait on loan from the Crown.

Prams bump through the gathered citizens here to see
the Master, and I can tell he's one who knows his worth,

but is his haggard face one of regret? After a certain age who
doesn't fight it? Throughout his life, he painted himself often,

painted his face four times in his last year. An X-ray of this
self-portrait reveals two pentimenti: his beret was made smaller

and darker, and from his hands he removed the tool, a paintbrush.
A Macedonian proverb says *Once you catch your bear*

it will dance for you, but no one buys a self-portrait. In his studio,
with a poodle, with helmet, and finally this rough, illuminated face

dancing for us his aged grief, or is it wisdom? Both?
We all see it, shining up the room. I read about his modest

parentage, three of his four children dead, his wife too
by age thirty. Bankruptcy and auction, his own illness.

But what does he paint when he paints his face?
The search for meaning brings us all down hard,

boom, to the knees, and maybe it's good to stay there
for a while and stare. It's where anger slew

citizenry, where love was used up for anyone
but your own, where people burned neighborhoods,

where many are broke or old or ill, where someone
wracks the night for a version of home, where a man

paints his own tired face. Rembrandt looks at himself
who looks at me. *Once you catch your bear*

it will dance for you only works if you're the bear,
only if the suffering in you rises to meet the suffering

in the other. I've no child with me today, no one to hurry me
back into the flurry of snack, birds, Kings Bridge, Sunnyside

to home. I'll leave Belfast before marching season for reasons
of family, visas, and money though I'll wish I could stay by then.

Rembrandt died penniless for reasons of appetite (oh, he lived!),
and he was buried in a debtor's grave. No, please, not regret.

*

No rest until Ireland is united, says he, the young one,
assured, calm. His grandfather and father's fight will be

his own and so on. The empty folding tables are surrounded
by empty folding chairs, and sugar sloughs across the desk

where tea was made. I write it down—upstairs office
and butcher shop below, the murals of masked men

with machine guns, the razor-wired gardens. *We'll not forget.*
I want to know more, what is this kind of remembering?

I know this fever, intractable. The symbolic thrives in Belfast:
a melancholic dove nests in barbed wire twined with slogans.

The wall behind is painted light blue and white, presenting
that rarest thing, a sunny day; a memorial lit from 10 p.m. to dawn.

William, a musician, says, *It's in our* (whose?) *DNA to march,
we must parade.* The example is his (Protestant) niece

who tantrums to march on St. Patrick's Day. *A fecking diplomat*,
mutters Mícheál who visibly shrugs it off. *In those days*

*people face-to-face playing music with you one day, the next
might bomb your car.* He rolls another cigarette, brushes

the tobacco off, heads home to carry his sick wife to bed.

*

The shore of sleep recedes too far, and I pass
from bedroom to living room to kitchen for water

or magazine through the dark wreckage of house,
light now on against it. The computer glows blue and I

find stories of people I once knew or heard of,
the vast public scrapbook about joy, politics, lunch,

grief, that spit curl she had when they first
married or how terrible the campaign coverage,

then an article of how Chekhov, after his brother died
of consumption and he himself began to cough,

went to a remote Russian island in the North Pacific
where murderers were sent to suffer exile with each other

and prison gates were always open to clean,
swept yards, because where else could they go?

Festival poster, shoehorn, fish clock with moving eyes,
a gilded plate kitschy and commemorative of Belfast's

Titanic, new silver stove, and, inside the glowing
box of screen, everything else. Chekhov, dying,

wanted a place that was *not ours, not Russian*, to make
the unknown known. The woman who sold pickled cabbage

had buried her infant, thinking she would get off easy
because he was alive when she put him in the ground.

Or that's what she said. Anton, what stories made sense
on Sakhalin Island? There the imprisoned married, starved,

and bore their skin-and-bones children. Chekhov writes,
In order as far as possible to visit all the inhabited spots,

and to become somewhat closer acquainted with the life
of the majority of the exiles, I resorted to a device which,

in my position, seemed the only way. I carried out a census.
Is this what I am doing? What complicity is this? D kicks

the wall in her sleep. She loves the coldness of old brick.

*

The groomed Botanic Gardens, a walk through
drizzle, and up the hill blinks the Palm House, an ornate

Victorian glass house with layers of flowers, the floor
littered with petals. D asks if she can gather those

because she has been told the living blooms are for everyone.
We enter the Tropical Ravine (another antique idea)

from its second story and look down into a humid forest
with thick koi circling, mottled, inbred. A couple of broken

panes of glass let in a chill rain, which pierces the steam.
A sparrow and a long-tailed tit settle in, exotic against the foliage,

their grays and browns made vivid by wide banana leaves
and bromeliads with scarlet spears. Every day we attempt

to name the birds and other things as we walk to school
down the bunkerish stairwell of the building to the fog-swathed

morning of Belfast. Graffiti, check. Empty cider bottles, check.
Dog shit, slush of vomit, double check. A magpie bounds.

For luck, we ask it, *Howdy, Captain, how's the missus?*
Facades of buildings are doctored up to look unempty.

Just beyond their windows the many terraced houses
are ruined on the inside, still, after years. D is lately

learning to fly, leaping sincerely from the porch,
the pleats in her school uniform filled with air.

Sometimes we two conduct a study of mosses
ubiquitous; sometimes we simply run. At the park's entrance,

at the first twisted, moss-covered, monstrous, seductive,
horizontally-inclined old tree, there is a billboard set off

in shrubbery with images of women dancing,
a Chinese lion (nostrils so circular), fish, and Chinese characters.

In English: *Share the Beauty of this Graceful Moonlight.*
D chants it when she thinks of lions, of China,

the moon, or a deep green park. Mid-Autumn Festival is the time
to find your people or return home. Or rather, even when

miles away, we admire the same moon (the harvest
is mostly metaphorical), the same lonely beauty.

*

We've all done it—wanted something much and more
than given and so Aoife, the stepmother, became jealous

of Fionnuala and her brothers, the children of Lir,
jealous of the ruddy smiles pouring for them from

the king's face. She sees how even the sun is in love
with the baby's hair, the baby still carried on his hip.

Aoife could not bear her king's love shared nor
divided. It's a kind of greed, that love, not really

a love at all. We've all seen it. I once had a friend
who told me things, poems, secrets; we were pregnant

together with girls, our beautiful girls. She gave me
trinkets, precious secrets, then took them away

all at once. I grieved, was furious. I thought I'd found
a fellow traveler in this world outside my class.

All that I've left behind—an early marriage, hard
labor, my people, my clan—for this writing of poems,

owning of property, with teeth white, well tended. My friend,
too, had traveled a long way. When her face turned mask,

I remembered my own turning and all my awful goodbyes.
I wondered what she had not told me, not once,

of what she'd wanted. Now, from Belfast, I recognize anew
(with less passion this time) what it takes to change

a life, its circumstance. Here, neighborhoods (Catholic)
bear their murals of Che, Dr. Martin Luther King Jr., or

Mother Teresa to remind us how to do it without greed.

*

The dead will walk, though the news often surprises.
After the burial of his father a friend discovers a letter

concerning compensation for "shell shock." I met a man
who studied which soldiers suffered more in combat

than their fellow troops and why. Paid by the state, he did it
so the next young soldier would be able to kill without this
    suffering.

He had a rugged nickname, my friend's dad, tried to integrate
a Kentucky school as principal. My grandmother's brothers

drank themselves out of war, the POW camp, home, all.
Ditch-dead and done and here again they come, those dead,

refusing their condition, memory animating what's left
of flesh, of history. And what about mine? I nail wood

to windows, arm myself, and try to forget their stagger
and moans. There's a soldier with bloodied knees, and a soldier

with enough to move on. And where do I go?
To a country, this one, where the ghost of atrocity

lingers amidst the rows of terraced houses and good,
decent people. They who might not forget but are treaty bound

to forgive. Is this why I came? Surely not the weather.

*

A friend calls from America to discuss the campaign
and I say, *I can't, don't want to give those people*

my attention, not even that. Another discusses the job
I left behind and I say, *Stop.* All over, the news

is not good. Another says, *I know why you love Belfast,*
you are working class, too. Maybe, but easy for me

to say, *No, not anymore.* Easy as rasping the straw against the hole
in the soda can without thinking, or thinking about

some other crap. In an American city, another young man
is shot by officers, and I watch the footage, can't not

see his stagger into the street, the bullets that rend
his body even after he is down. Easy as chewing the

straw, pressing plastic between teeth, then, look,
a twisted, dead root of a thing. And then my election,

all Belfastians from piper to poet to binman
are puzzled by my candidates (mine?), want me to explain

the awfulness further revealed, revealing, about my people.
And these people, are they mine? No. Easy for me,

my foggy-head resistance, the neighbor saying
blah blah predictable about kindness or the nothingness

outside of God's love, easy to close the door, again,
Thank you! Or easy to say it's easy. Who am I?

Easy for me to leave for a city where I feel I can
disappear, one mostly desirous of not being divided,

to leave behind a country in which the hunted still
hang from the walls in an ancient idea of splendor.

*

In the story by Saki, one neighbor poaches while
the other hunts him, that interloper in his forest,

his inheritance, a forest east of the Carpathians,
his jealously guarded wood. With guns drawn, the two

meet on a stormy night. She did not mean well,
the queen of Lir, when she gathered the children up,

took them in her chariot to Lake Derravaragh
one hot day. We know why the children went so happily.

She was happy. She finally wanted them,
wanted to be the one who sits and watches while they

scatter fish, even as waterbirds flurry for cover, as if love
need do nothing more than see. And so the water shone,

the sun spilled itself purely for no reason
but goodness, and the shoreline swayed with heat,

and the stepmother used her magic to turn four children
into swans. Like that. They dove in and out of waves

while their thin arms grew flight feathers and
their freckled faces turned white, eyes to blackberries,

and Aoife declared they should swim as swans
three hundred years on this lake, three hundred

on the narrow Sea of Moyle, and three hundred
more on the Western Sea that does not end except

at sky. In my nighttime storytelling to myself, I play
different roles in this tale. I am the betrayed,

those children so transformed by loss they lose
their own bodies. I imagine myself into the queen

whose rage will not spare another person anything
because I know what it is to be full of hunger, an interloper.

Then I am the stupid, once happy king. Saki, who cannot
help but see the world through irony, pins his hunters under

a fallen tree the moment before each could shoot
the other. What blaze of lightning! What broken branches,

blinded eyes, bloodied. And then, trapped, the two
decide in favor of peace, of a better, mutual future, and,

as the rattle of rescue approaches, they unclench,
decide to forgive in each their decades of greed.

Saki, of course, ends this story not with the anticipated
rescue but with a pack of wolves, hungry, often found

in those forests, but I think of the peace they decided
and wonder if it would have held. Who does not love

to hate the betrayer? And who can say they are able
to gift her (in the nighttime storytelling to themselves)

all roles, the whole, truer range of selves: victimhood,
guilt, implication, and clean, sweet grief? As well as greed?

Belfast's murals, call them evidence. Set the martyr along
the Uzi; King Billy across from Bobby Sands; Ghandi's face,

Che's over from those dead in the Great War, a Protestant
cause lately. They seem a gilded conversation, a call

and response. UFF and UDA members lit with gold,
a smallish *Guernica* repurposed here, and Her Majesty

the Queen over there. RIP Stevie McCrae, a Red Hand
Commando; Oliver Cromwell's ahover over armored thugs

who've slain the fallen, foreshortened, at my feet;
Who gave their lives for Freedom, or boys in parkas

with guns. A scholar says a mural lets you know
you're home, among and safe in your tribe. The Ulster flag,

Union Jack, Tricolor. The Scottish flag and the Ulster crossing
behind two men at ease in masks with guns; the words

You smug faced crowds with kindling eye beside a portrait
wreathed in poppies, surveyed by a man in white coat, with mask,

with gun; six men's and women's faces comprise a frame,
inside three soldiers stagger into golden light, two shoulder guns

and the middle one is wounded; shields of the four provinces
of Ireland and, above, a man with a gun, dated 1916; and

more flags. The murals of Belfast are tourist attractions—
a bloody hand, a tombstone, two poppy wreaths, no gun;

seventeen plastic bullets, each with a face, and eight of these
are children; for God and Ulster, two masked men with guns

and a soldier from World War I; two men in masks
who brandish flags instead of guns; Irish Volunteers, a last

breakfast, guns at rest on table's lip; *Quis Separabit*—
"who will separate us"—a face and flags only. *He commenced*

his hunger strike . . . and tragically died on Sunday afternoon
2 Aug 1981 Kieran was elected T.D. by the people

of Cavan and Monaghan in their support of the prisoners
campaign for political status; a portrait of a striker

in the light of love, aglow, hair flowing, his shirt snowy.

*

The visitation of the jovial, American ambassador to Belfast
presents rhetoric, *You are the future. The twenty-first century*

is interconnectedness. The oil spill off Argentina poisons
reefs in Bali, et cetera. Yes, connected, all right. I drift off

and away. The Glass House and Bertie? Sure! The burly
security man with a Playboy bunny tattoo rising above

his collar and my friends waking in America
to doves cooing their Armageddon of mating and dying,

mating, dying. The Great Hall is great—mostly murky portraits
of men—see that one man in an armchair, lap smothered

in Shih Tzu. There's the pervasive bard of the North,
"Famous Seamus" they call him when they want to be naughty,

which is usually. The few women haggardly hold their ground,
portraits featuring every wrinkle, their gray, wiggish hair.

Who could tell any of these people from their portraits?
I nod in respect to the women (sorry, Edna! It's you!),

to those I don't know, whose impressive thoughts
and deeds got them into these dignified frames.

I take a photo with the ambassador, *Where are you from?*
et cetera. Stand closer. Then home, to the shop and the hurry

to St. Brid's for the fiddle lesson. The cabdriver I find
much easier to talk to, lived in New York, a migrant

bricklayer. Seeing D's fiddle case, he brags, *My grandfather
MacIntyre was a champion fiddler.* MacIntyres are Scottish,

most of them Protestants, maybe. "Telling" is the Belfast trick
I too have begun to practice. Myth has a MacIntyre

cutting off a thumb to plug a hole in his ship. *Hands too big
for fiddling*, he says, and they are large, rough on the wheel.

He says all the tradespeople are driving cabs, as he is,
and overcharging when they do get building work

so no one's hiring Irish. *Poles, isn't that another story*,
he snorts. *The poorer we are, the more we fight. It's the scarcity.*

St. Brid's locked up, no fiddle tonight, and D hardly sorry.

*

Either the children of Lir are lost or they appear before their
     father,
fanning his brow, singing in their true voices for him—

the tale chooses the latter, of course. Either the king sees them
for who they are or thinks it all a trick of longing, since

such sweet words do not come from birds. But we love
that he knows them. Their soft feathers and curved necks are
     what

he dreams of now, when he sleeps on the shores of the lake.
D asks, *But what happened to the stepmother, where did she go?*

As if she could not live after doing this. D's yet to learn
it's not impossible. Either Aoife confesses her story to the king

or lies to him of a storm, their drowning, but either way
I know she feels faint with dread, eventually incinerates

all signs of self until she cannot be anything but a bitter wraith,
a spirit beyond despair. *And so she ended her beauty in the gray*

narrows of morning, I tell my child, *became a fury of wind*
for the rest of all time upon the surface of Lake Derravaragh.

*

A root of balm, a root of bane, the news pronounces
for the day. I call it all painful. Wind flays the trees

beside the river D and I cross to get to school, library,
the rest of the world, and an old oak has had too much,

reared itself, shown its mess, its new logic of naked root,
black earth, and death. The levels of betrayal seem infinite

in Donal's new article about the IRA, the Army, peace-
makers. I am lost tracking them, won't anymore today.

Back home, the flute of chimney blows a wild tune
I don't want to know. *Christ*, I say, *don't we cover up*

these things? The chill wafts from between bricks
inexplicably. A body absorbs all kinds of mystery,

cold, the pavement, the father shot, teeth pulled out
with pliers, the gorgeous image of torn root, a wet

of blood, an officer sleeping in a car and the vivid hedge
beyond. Today's storm is named Henry. Before that, Gertrude,

Frank, and Eva. Desmond, Clodagh, Barney, and finally
Abigail. There is no personage for this stew, this day,

and now the soaked child wants her tea. No illuminating
anecdote to pass us through yet more gust and confusion.

Noli me tangere is what Jesus said to Mary Magdalene
when she recognized him after his death. Maybe the Greek

translates better, *Cease holding on to me*. Men in reflective vests and city coveralls touch the broken bits strewn about

on grass, the gnarled oak's under. I wish it gone tomorrow.

*

As we are walking into Belfast city center a flock
of communion dresses, sparkled and white, preen

in a store window. D asks what they are and I tell her,
It's a uniform for a ceremony that some children do.

I did it, was welcomed into the Catholic Church.
She says, *Like presenting.* Yes. *I loved my dress,* I say,

*the little pearl necklace was sewn to either side of the zipper
so I would not lose it ever.* D wants it, dress and pearls.

Sorry, it's long gone, sweetheart. So much gone, leaving
that church behind—it stuns me suddenly.

The glittering passage of sacrament, the book that,
with careful attention, revealed what any person needs

to organize this pain, this thick and often broken beauty,
this world's (and my own) selfishness and virtue.

Then D asks me, *Are we union?* I say, *Unionist?*
Another child asked you this? Later, at a dinner party

a woman growls that her sister married this guy and
she can't stand him, a black bastard. *Black? Yes,* she steps in

closer, *a true Protestant arsehole.* Sign in a stairwell:
Mind Your Head. Sign in the park: No Dog Fouling.

Titanic Belfast (interactive museum) has a narrow
bottom flaring to a fluted prow. It's a silver cup

filled with steel and words and words. Stevie snarks,
The boat was fine when she left. In Belfast conspiracy

is never far. A German with a cap by a glass case points
his children to the piles of plates rimmed in gold, pulled

from a frozen sea, now lit and ready to be consumed.
Catholics (mostly) washed linen then, we read, children

rescued the shuttles. Protestants melted with volcanic flame
one monstrous sheave of metal to its mate. *By spacing*

the warp more closely, one can completely cover the weft
that binds it. Words and words. D is supremely bored,

too many words floating above objects made unavailable
to her senses by curatorial notions of representation.

Interactive? Bah! I say to D as I take her with me
to the finish, leaving the in-laws and husband behind.

On the way out, a woman in a photo, strange dress and shoes,
watches workers on break. I study her empty buckets

and wonder about her days, tasks, pains. What did she bring?
Some kind of lunch for her workers? Water? A boy

shirtless and shoeless is about to toss a stone at a horse.
Today, I am the boy. Meanwhile, the empty-faced man

on Botanic Avenue completes his one-thousandth shift
before the Mexican restaurant with a name unrecognizable

as Spanish. *Any process that uses a localized heat source
such as welding is likely to result in some distortion.*

His overtime hours are filled in front of Russell's,
watch cap and hood, always grim. He shifts on a crate,

cardboard placematting his soles, never once asking
for coins, food, love, the time, so don't offer it.

He will meet your eyes directly; his are clear, calm
about his position in the world of this city street.

*A handloom weaver would propel the shuttle by throwing it
from side to side, aided by a picking stick.*

Jane from Australia says so many men she's met or dated
are wounded by the Troubles. PTSD, secrecy, boundaries

solidified into selvesful of suspicion. A City Hall mural
says Belfast lost a third of its population during the Troubles,

and who could blame them? Who stayed is the better question.
I study how the man shuffles through his plastic bag

of newspaper clippings while his crate tipped over reveals
the slots for bottles are filled with more bits of newspapers

I can't quite see nor, when I try, imagine. Day after day,
he plows forward through nothing more discernable to me

than the day. When it's raining, which is often, he moves his crate
under the awning. And starts up the work of being, right there.

*

I wake. I am older, old enough to not be quite
beautiful, my skin no longer smooth. I could say

I used to, I used to, but that desire too is fading. I've dyed
my hair the brown it used to be and can hear my husband

making coffee in the kitchen. D must be writing in her room
as she often does because I don't hear her singing one of her

made-up songs, like "Happy Day to the Prisoners!" Arias
in a private opera. I ponder all the stories she shares. Today,

a fawn is separated from her beautiful mother, chased
by both bear and hunter, then rescued by friendly chipmunks.

Reunited, doe and fawn have a good laugh. She's come to read it
to me, begins as I lug myself up onto the pillows. H whistles

while he putters, as usual; the music drowns in the kettle's noise.

*

It was our privilege to serve, said the man,
but, now, what was it for? According to his parents

the RC were the scourge. I am not sure what RC is, and then
I know it's me and mine in some distant, watermark-

on-vellum way. Victims Services serve us all, grief
is grief. *So now they say they are the victims?*

growls the man who lost his father on the Falls Road
though he doesn't remember him, really.

He came out of the school where the RC teachers learned
to teach and likely it was cloudy and wet that day

and the smell of the rain was nil, because there is so much.
No cars, that day, only rain and wind. *In and out the dusty*

bluebells, in and out the dusty bluebells, who shall be my partner?
his primary class might have sung as they waited for mums.

The babies sodden in their prams, the toddlers meandering
off and on the pavement, mums approached in dribs and drabs.

He will not be able to recall his father in a few years.
His brothers will take their mother to a neutral part of south
    Belfast,

a widow the rest of her days. But that day, the primary class
quieted and the mums smoked and they parted for his.

She had the poise of a medieval Madonna,
a perfection of grief one can only feel the way

toward. The mums touched her, offered food,
help. *Husbands are fragile*, she said. *We are not.*

She was the Joan of Arc, the Medea, the Mother
and the Father, the Pincher, the Wall, the Grabber,

the Feeder, the Slapper, the Wiper, the Crumbs off
the Table and No Toilet in the House, the Pirm,

the Arc-Flame, the Linen, and the Steel, says he.

*

A cabdriver told us the British soldiers performed black magic
in the tower where they watched all the city. Magic?

There is no other explaining for it, says he. *They all did.*
Both sides. Evilness from both, but I'll not be saying more.

The conversations with cabdrivers are direct, seem honest—
the intimacy of the drive, faces meeting in a rearview mirror,

the anonymous flurry of laying it all out for the uninformed
American so clearly without a dog in the fight. D tells a driver

that she plays fiddle in the Rose & Crown. *I can't go there,*
says he, *they'd hit me ON THE HEAD. I'm pure Sandy Row.*

Then I notice his graffitied hands and neck. Much adored
at the Rosie, our lovely girl has never imagined this danger.

She stares at me for answers. Later, her father tells her
that long ago there was a bomb at that pub during a fight

and it killed people. Once I told a driver he had brought us home
before (his tweeds and pipe a bit storybook, hard to forget,

he ejected us and our groceries with a perfect *Oot ye go, luv*),
which he, side-eyed, denied and spoke no more.

*

Was there ever a movie lover who was not a great sensualist?
writes a critic about film noir. *My black wig on the chair,*

writes a poet of the dark, grainy life she used to have
organized by drugs, poverty, crime—that old trinity.

I drank to forget, why else? Rob said about the past, and so it was
a distance from which to wave, distracted, genial, at all the rest.

The blur of voices, the spill and slosh, the bed, again, and we
did not stop him, and some suggested nothing but patience,

and the blood transfused, dark and glowing like the paint
his wife spilled on the deck, the old wood that drank it drank

without trying, so old and thirsty, as empty of desire as the dog
who has loosened itself from kindness or heat, anything but

the catastrophe of hunger, because there's a small arrow inside
any animal, its point golden and sharp against the swallowed

organs—he maybe put it there, or was given one by a family,
maybe by this lonely war—but dulling it is one way to save

us, chock it down blear the drag the dog can't eat such a stupid hope
mange rot he fashioned himself bottlesful of regret, a word no

one should be afraid of anymore. I'm certainly not these days.
It's no fallacy to regret, even as I know I did not or could

not have done anything else, and here's to the wait, for all of us,
the purple flowers spot the yellow skin, the hard piercing from

underneath, and the flowers are not good or simple or beautiful,
and then didn't he ask to curry the ponies, to play music,

old tunes, and curry the ponies, and the last of the words didn't
mean a thing, mere broken glass across neurons, to anyone,

not me, not us, the pour was on the inside now, as he was lifted
from driveway to car, to be sustained by the beep and tube

and fat envelopes of wine-red stuff, which preserve the heart
and the lungs for others who will be so grateful, as we

are grateful for him, the other one, not the flat mass on the screen
whose borders are loose and growing. There's a black wig

on the chair for you. Surely the sensualist's relationship
to history is often pain and the world is full of us.

D, choosing to write her report on Harriet Tubman, describes
Tubman's head injury, filling many of the required pages

with inordinate bloody detail in her grief for another
human's wound. One sadness was that, says D,

Harriet didn't know her birthday. No one wrote it down.

*

The children of Lir are not immune. It's not impossible
that they would dream of robes they used to wear, not

these ragged feathers. Fionnuala can't protect them from grief
(who can?), from wanting to go back before this violence

of beak and claw, this huddle on a wild sea far away from
kin. After the second three hundred years of their spell, the children

flew over a castle where a party sparkled. See the gentle
folk dance forward on white horses, and, oh my, we rode

beasts such as these. Smell the food on spits in the kitchen yard,
smoke rising, mingling with the thick spumes from chimneys,

and, oh, twenty or more chimneys had we. One brother swan
flying through the haze called, *Aren't you our comrades,*

the people we knew? Isn't this our castle? Aren't we home
at the mouth of our own river? Tell us, how is our father?

Oh, that King has flown, said the Fairy Host as he led the ghosts,
for that is what they were, back into the castle, which then

crumbled to dust. Thus begins the nostalgia for hope, the glow
of trap, the no more go around, the snap of broken. Thus begins

the final surrender. *Sure, let's sit at the table, feast with ghosts.*

*

A series of clicks and I find an essay, a painful (for me) tale
featuring my own home in a remote wooded state, a hotel

where my nephew worked before addictions staggered him,
where a writer stayed with her baby. Excessive attention

ensued. My people and I are, after all, villagers, and in that web
of familiarity, generations of relation, we get too curious

from not knowing. The writer from California browses
a local real-estate magazine, says she can't imagine

what it's like to live in houses that are so cheap, the houses
in which I grew up, my family, those hotel maids too.

I am pierced—is this shame, anger, both? I mumble all
the rest of the day about houses, what makes them cheap.

While combing D's hair, blond, wispy, touching her curls,
I think about the writer's girl, how people wanted to touch her hair,

an African American child's hair, hair unfamiliar to them,
and how this line is crossed from a deep lack of connection

that they'd just touch a stranger's hair, a child's. What is my grief
reading this, really? That I know at one time I might have

done the same, touched the baby's hair, and was that racism or
desire? Both. And would the writer care that when she spoke of

cheap houses, I who'd once served food at another hotel nearby
would feel a resentment so piercing I had to click the screen shut?

Not hard to see how even strangers could become so fiercely
and not at all abstractly estranged, harder to imagine speaking

across years, birth, and fear. Batten, button, zip right up.
    Meanwhile,
here in the paper, an anniversary: "We in the Easter Rising
    Committee

would like to make it clear that we are unrepentant Irish republicans
who uphold the right of those who took on the might

of the British Empire to do so by force of arms. We make
no apologies for that. We will not be inviting unionists, loyalists

or any manifestation of the British state to our commemorations."
The unionists had already turned the invitation down.

*

Was Judas's sin that he betrayed Jesus or that he sent
any man at all to his death? Does it matter more *who* was harmed?

The ex-paramilitary said it was more important who the person
was you'd shot, rather than why you did it. I can't

believe him, couldn't it simply be a whisper, some coins
and simple greed? There's a fresco of Judas hanged

in Notre Dame des Fontaines—see his companion,
a small, winged monkey-devil with two faces,

one where a face should be and the other on his anus.
I brought back from France a postcard of this Judas

more than twenty years ago. It still pulls at me.
It asks me, *Who can you hate more than yourself?*

It begs me, *Who can you forgive?* It warns, *Don't be too
astonished at your own black wings.* The police tape

halts your lift home from the airport. The paper
details the assassination two streets over the night before,

a late supper interrupted by invasion, the attempt to hide
in the bathroom, the bullets through the door. Warned

upon his release from prison, he hid four months
from his own people, says a cabdriver who's in the know.

It was his own crew that done it. I know his father.
The boy had it coming. The textbooks say each killed

an equal number of their own, are still doing it, in small
starts and stops. Judas's little devil digs through his gut

toward a smaller version of Judas himself, who's birthed
from the sluice of organs on my time-tired postcard.

We tell D that the police tape is due to sewer damage as
there'd be no way to answer or stop the awful questions.

Judas wept, but what's born from his belly is an infant,
a smaller version of *himself* who leaps into the devil's arms.

And what did we do when ours was born, so dear we could
have licked her like a cat, loved her like a guitar? Everywhere

I consented to her face, in the blue of that broken bottle,
that sliced foot, in shrubbery twisted and cut into porpoises

breaching a damp lawn—what if all of you were outside
your body, your best and worst bejeweled by dew, witnessed

by impersonal commuters, teachers, delivery people?
What were you thinking, bringing a child into this knowing

called the world? What could she learn from you, one
who deep inside your murky soul agrees it matters

who was shot, that you'd do awful things to save her.

*

I walk along the Lagan, which splits the town,
the light at 9 p.m. a strange glory. Jeff, poet,

seems to make the birds appear and names them all,
a tall, blond advertisement for the peaceable kingdom.

That slight, greased shape? I see it, say it, *A seal!*
He, direct, very American, denies my call—fresh

water, shallow river, how? Later, at the book launch
on a grounded barge, no one thinks it's impossible.

So Irish of the poets to go there with my wondrous tale
while giving me shit for a corny image all at once.

The students at D's school believe it too. In my poetry
lesson we talk about how truth is sometimes better

as a story or in a poem. Nigel is the student I thought he'd be,
the square peg dreaming, Olu a wiggly distraction,

and the girls that D likes best are perfect in their attention.
The world is made from fire and we're not humans,

Nigel's voice rises. *We are little flaming things instead*
The world has no roads but we can fly

Instead of water we have lava, we have no floors
Instead of dogs we have fire titans on chains

This is a whole new universe
This place is called the nether

*

I read about Denis Donoghue, scholar, a Catholic son
of the North, his insistence on Irish identity as the only

critical subject available, an idea that makes sense
in the deep dark night while my family is sleeping.

During bedtime procedures, *You are always
contradicting me.* D, right back, *No I'm not.*

H came back from music at Madden's, said the mural
of Fionn mac Cumhaill scared him in the dark

as if a twenty-foot person had suddenly appeared before him.
Donoghue's relationship to Yeats was his most important,

says a critic, Yeats the Protestant through which Donoghue
sees the world that to him is utterly Catholic. What of that?

How we too much see ourselves in the other? How this night
in Belfast tells me more than anything American can. Another

page turned and Colm Tóibín describes how he realized slowly
and without pain two things: that he was an atheist

and that a united Ireland was not worth marching for.
One of the reasons that Henry James Sr. offered neighbors

for *gathering his young family up and taking them
constantly to Europe was that their sensuous education*

was not being properly looked after in the US.
What a glory to not be so American tonight.

I feel it in my ear, in the names of fiddle tunes—"Spinster's Reel,"
"Munster Buttermilk," "The Banshee," "Humours of Tulla"—

or when a grown man says, "Daddy," or when questions
turn into negatives, *You wouldn't be wanting to head*

to the Errigle? It's my language and not my language,
a subtle retuning of thought itself. And poor Tóibín,

poor me mostly, what is left after no god and no
cause? After betrayal? After exile, after true hate,

after loss, a dying planet, another long night of the soul?
A self to improvise from shining bits and pieces: the books

I love, I write, the velvet voices of grown-ups that comfort
D in the next room, the fiddles asleep in their solemn cases,

the smell of chimney smoke on a colder night.
Studying with Denis Donoghue was for Tóibín the first

serious, concentrated glimpse of a sensuous universe,
what remains for him and for me too. Behold family,

the house, this book. Behold sensuous pillow, fog, streetlight,
the tiled flowers circling the hearth. Tonight is this universe.

*

The epistemology of, nature and scope, the hedge
the boundary of garden, bog field, the high field,

and the paddock field. Won't you dissect the field
of knowledge of the Modern Mistress stove, the wee tap

on the side, granny had one in the very spot closest
to Scotland (eighteen miles) in all the North, or the presuppositions

of her liberty bodice, knobs and straps for attaching
more and other undergarments? Let's interrogate the extent

and validity of the glass churn with wooden paddles
a mother cranked and then each sister cranked until

butter. What are the sufficient conditions of the two up,
two down, a narrow stair to the attic? Are they attacked by

the justified belief in anything metal, wood, or flesh?
The holly stand out back? The creation and dissemination

of a Soldier's New Testament (Psalms in meter), his proudest
item still, though it's said testimony does not have its own

faculty and, according to evidentialism, there is
materialist proof of all the Belfasts and their existence,

the existence of her French doll, wooden and hollow
as a spool, the crown of nails for knitting. Luminosity

of cognition is this antler pocketknife purchased with leftover
wedding money whilst on a honeymoon on the Golden Mile,

and let's just call this noble photo of her father in his brass-button uniform true, if only by accident or testimony or love.

*

And weren't they at it all night, the greengrocer asks
as he picks two pounds fifty from my palm. I'm buying

more strawberries for D's lunch since the clever older girl
at school usually ends up with most of them somehow.

Scottish are best, the girl advises. The fog was cool that morning
and the webs on the hedges knit with dew. His hands are the size

of shovels, clean and meaty as he wraps a pint of (Irish) berries.
I like his tenderness toward fruit, mock scowl for the skies.

A neighbor says he's too nice; it makes her feel odd—
a very Belfast thing to say. Everyone here can read

the veg man but me, Catholic, Protestant, blow-in, too nice?
Even potatoes have a provenance in this country.

It's all too human to organize a universe. He couldn't believe
I chose to live in Belfast, laughed when I said we came back.

Those spiders were at it all night. Can you believe it? It couldn't
be the extra dew? *No, it's a feckin' insect conspiracy.*

During the morning walk, D let me carry her backpack and coat.
Hers is the Protestant school where twenty-one languages

are spoken, an immigrant school. Rabbit quick, she ran into
the fog by the playing fields, shouting, *Take a picture of me*

disappearing! then reemerged not alone, but with Nigel, who
wanders to school when we do, his glasses askew, Star Wars

backpack dragging. The children sprinted the muddier path gladly (*Tip! You're it!*) while the grass glowed with dew and

indeed everywhere, a conspiracy traced with water, light.

*

After nine hundred years. After the last flight where they heard
no wavecrash, no horsesnort nor mudsquelch nor

wingflap but their own. After they flew Home. After the hills
were strangely brown and all the castles a sigh of ruin.

After the forests were gone. After they believed there
was nothing to return to. After they met a stranger man and

after he threw himself to the ground crying, *Oh mighty birds
have you come from Tir-na-Og?* After they begged him

to say why all the mountains died, and he told them
to put their ears to any old, worn slope and listen.

After the mountain whispered, *I am yet alive.* After they
returned to their human bodies. After the children met the saint

who was a slave. After the bell in his church called the start
of prayer. After they were laid on the banks of the River Bann.

After their flesh became dust. After the stranger man
kept their story well, which is why D and I read it now.

*

As of late too much in the past, a neighbor asks,
What is a quiet mind? His handsome face reveals he is

genuinely confused. I know that it's not merely
rhetorical this question, not for him. Answering

reveals my many inadequacies. Vivian Gornick
writes about rereading "Howards End" forty years later,

how this time she saw that Forster, age thirty-one, didn't
know love when he wrote it, but knew he must write

toward the mystery. *What is a quiet mind?* That Gornick
feels pity for Forster comforts me, that a reader may pity me.

If I ever find a working definition of a quiet mind
I will let everyone know. The neighbor says, *It will end*

only when we die. Only his generation's demise
allows everyone to move on? That we are too much

changed by event, grief, history, maybe anger and failure
so much our darknesses that all we can do is wait

in our quiet homes, unpeaceful until the end? I have tried
to quiet my mind this year, worked a patient spinning in place,

taking notes on what I see and don't, the mystery, studying
my frail nostalgia for when I bore a more open soul.

I don't get that back, do I? But I would not have loved
Belfast so well in my trusting days. At this middle stage

cruelty becomes the abiding mystery. Images for a quiet mind
haunt—a door flung open, the green hills of Donegal,

or Fermanagh, an infant swaddled in clean linen,
the dove of peace as Matisse printed it, simply, purely

white against a thick blue. We all want to hold it and
we want it weightless, warm, sublime. Who will rend

this quiet from the world and place it inside you?
Would you know it's there? Here's a photograph of Matisse

at my neighbor's age now, almost eighty, white beard,
wool cap and robe, seated below the photographer.

To the right, white birds, nearly transparent with sunshine,
perched on top of an open cage. On the left at his elbow,

an empty one. Behind, in the shadow, another cage, full
or empty I can't see. A bird is in Matisse's hands;

he holds it like a sandwich. Seeing this I feel it,
why doves mean peace. It might not even be a dove

but it rests in his hands easily, with trust. Am I ready
for quiet? Picasso had said of Matisse, his friend,

that when one of them died there'd be all sorts of things
the other would never say to anyone again.

*

Gerard scowls across the breakfast table at the sole drinker
who's risen when the hour is decent. If the furrow

in a forehead could become a weapon, then
my husband is dead. Gerard, a Pioneer, took "the pledge"

years ago, as in swore off booze forever,
a Catholic rite of passage. H sips tea and fields

questions, oh so many questions, about his parents,
education, faith (Unitarian). Later in the States,

telling Berni, he laughs with her about her dad.
The gorgeous suburbs are fat and green with summer.

The children play basketball, done with their fiddle lessons,
dinner, ice cream with sprinkles. Jazz piano

uncontained by the maze of backyard shrubs,
the boundaries that do not say boundary, drifts

compliments of Jo and Ike who played in South Side
nightclubs long ago, while Gus the bulldog patrols

the perimeter only for toddlers, odors, butterflies.
Athletic, smart, Berni's American husband Matt

says, *I wouldn't go for marching season again.*
Men in terrible uniforms and hats staggering down

the street playing the shitty music that comes
from playing once a year. Playing like amateurs.

Once we had to wait in hours of traffic for them
to finish. Berni says, *I never think of it these days.*

Who's Catholic, who is not. I don't know if my friends here
are anything at all. Then Matt, who played ball

for Loyola, finesses a driveway dunk full of grace,
emphasizing the sheer irrelevance of the question

in Forest Hills, the longest day of the year finally
letting go. Their three and our one conspire in the woodchips

by a spruce. *Oh look*, says Berni, *the roses have come.*

Achilles weeps over Hector's body, the body he had
killed for glory, revenge, to open the door to his own

prophesized, glamorous death. He weeps not for Hector
but for his own father and, truly, for himself. Priam weeps

over his son's gorgeous corpse, so gorgeous it won't rot.
I wish I didn't feel sorry for warriors, but I'm listening to

Derek Jacobi tell the story, his rich English voice filling my earbuds.
I approach the trees that line the Green, where men on ropes

climb with chain saws, trimming as they mount even higher
against the woolen sky. Their confidence in their task astounds.

I weep with Achilles while the arborists tie ropes to limbs
before they saw, to safely lower the hewn to the ground.

That gods immortal cannot age nor learn from their mistakes
breaks me every time, that one might not learn from suffering.

Later, while a drunk next door bangs the furniture
against the walls at midnight, doors open and close

on voices urgent, shrieking, disappearing down
the speed-bumped streets and curbsided bins that wait

for morning. O those young, leaping binmen, white
jumpsuits, impeccable gloves and hair, who will flicker

at dawn past lampposted sea birds, and O the collection
lorries, many-paneled vehicles that ladder the streets,

with starts and stops down each route to the river,
my trash to be piled on barges that will bear it

across many seas. I laugh at myself, binmen
as oracles, recycling as metaphor for my desire to start

over, or as metaphor for living. I am terrified
by the depth of D's sleep, which I cannot resist

interrogating, the heat of snore and drowse and
pillow snuffle, the dark cool outside the window,

the alleyway beacons, and the sterile offsiteness
of caution tape spillaging all our future griefs,

their management, and the ways we will all yet suffer.

*

Let there be a firmament in the midst of the waters,
and let it divide the waters from the waters, says

Genesis. Let there be a person in the midst of the city
and let the person divide the city from the city, I say.

Let there be one-legged birds of air to perch on branches
and let them confuse air with body. Let the cars trawl

the long rivers of streets to divide their houses
from our houses. A checkerboard of leaves stretches

across the street and a shadow of a sudden fills the window
and won't let go. Let there be a woman wandering

and why not let her separate anger from living. Let there be a child
in a bed that divides that bed from the rest of the world.

Let there be a deck of cards, food in the fridge,
a book about immigrants, a fiddle tune that can divide

a house from the world, also known as house.
Let the kitchen, its silver pots huddled on the shelf,

and the garden, where tomatoes sleep against newspaper
to save their fat heads, let it all save a slip of meaning from

the waters to be our firmament. Let there be one thing
that can divide fear from fear and the known from this only night.

*

Pieces of the end of a day, of my time here.
The charity solicitor uses the word *whilst* sincerely,

here they all do. And *whilst* I walk I am untangling myself
from a web of this against the moving fog, primitive

clouds that roll as if they must hurry to the ledge
of the horizon, hordes of them, animals urging each other

to the blind leap over the edge of black slate rooftops
across Sunnyside. I will not hurry. Brick, brick, yellow door,

black, black, red door. My daughter notices there is not
a single stop sign in our neighborhood. *Why don't we all crash?*

says she. *Feeling Peckish?* says the grocery wall. Everything
seems tangled in a knot of ending until we stop at the crosswalk.

The rain begins again. D presses the small yellow button
to halt the traffic so we may traverse the busy Ormeau Road.

I tell this small girl, *You have the most powerful finger in the world.*
But her power is not yet in question—the not-yet-wounded

wear faith easy and with finesse. As she races to the other curb,
D stomps a murky puddle as hard as she is able. All those messes,

houses, jobs, countries where we mend, make do and still
we crumble. And starting over might be this, a dear foot

a soaked shoe, skipping through. It's what you do that matters,
not all these feelings. What will she remember? What will you?

NOTES

Throughout this book, the names of the people whose stories and experiences I have presented have been changed for reasons of privacy, unless the person mentioned is a public figure in a public context.

8: *Silent Testimony* is the name of the Ulster Museum exhibit by Colin Davidson.

11: The piper mentioned is Paddy Keenan.

12: The quoted material in the telling of the Children of Lir comes from an especially lovely version in an online compendium of stories in the public domain: http://www.sacred-texts.com/neu/celt/cwt/cwt12.htm. In transit, we lost the book given to us, and I found words as lovely as that lost text here.

14: The zombie serial mentioned is *The Walking Dead*.

16: The painting referenced first is *Christian Flautists Outside St Patrick's* (2015), by Joseph McWilliams. The Ulster Museum received six complaints about it. The Rembrandt painting is *Self Portrait at the Age of 63* (1669).

18: I would like to express my gratitude to the outreach office of Sinn Féin for answering many questions.

19: The material quoted is from *Sakhalin Island*, by Anton Chekhov

(Bloomsbury, NY: Alma Classics, 2013).

30: "You smug faced crowds with kindling eye" is from Siegfried Sassoon's poem "Suicide in the Trenches." "*Quis Separabit*" is a motto associated with Ulster unionism and the British Army in Northern Ireland. All other quotations are from murals in Belfast.

32: Professor Edna Longley of Queen's University Belfast is the subject of the one portrait of a woman recognized in the poem. The other women honored in the Great Hall are Queen Victoria, President Mary McAleese, Professor Mary G. "Mollie" McGeown, Baroness May Blood, Lady Brenda McLaughlin, Professor Dame Ingrid Allen, and Professor Elizabeth Meehan.

35: "A root of balm, a root of bane" is from the Christina Rossetti poem "At Last."

38: The language to describe weaving has been adapted from various weaving websites, mainly https://wikivividly.com/wiki/Kissing_the_shuttle. The welding information is equally repeated across websites, such as https://www.twi-global.com.

41: "Dusty Bluebells" is a common children's song. It was featured in a BBC documentary from the 1970s that is worth watching: https://www.youtube.com/watch?v=UdpXTFy3zlw.

44: This poem is inspired by and draws from Suzanne Lummis's fine article "(Never) Out of the Past: Film Noir and the Poetry of Lynda Hull." The line quoted by Lummis and myself is from Hull's poem "Black Mare." The full article can be found here: https://lareviewofbooks.org/article/

never-out-of-the-past-film-noir-and-the-poetry-of-lynda-hull/.

47: The essay referenced presents the complicated history of race in Maine quickly and well. Camille Dungy is the writer. It can be found at http://www.nereview.com/vol-36-no-2-2015/camille-t-dungy/. The responsibility for the speaker's feelings about its content is mine, not the author's.

48: The quotation is from "Unionists unwelcome at our Easter Rising commemoration, says republican group," by Suzanne Breen, *Belfast Telegraph*, October 28, 2015.

51: The American named is Jeffrey Thompson, an extraordinary writer and traveler.

52: The material interpreted is from *Ireland and Transatlantic Poetics: Essays in Honor of Denis Donoghue*, ed. Brian G. Caraher and Robert Mahony (Newark: University of Delaware Press, 2007). The essay by Colm Tóibín that I reference is called "What to Do. How to Live." I take responsibility for any errors in interpretation.

59: The article referenced, "Song of Inexperience," is by Vivian Gornick and can be found at https://www.nytimes.com/2016/02/14/books/review/song-of-inexperience.html?_r=0.

Space travel timeline

Here are some highlights of our exploration of space with manned and unmanned spacecraft. Where will we go in the future?

International Space Station
The ISS is the largest structure in space, and has been occupied since November 2000.

Curiosity rover
This unmanned spacecraft has explored the surface of Mars since August 2012.

Seven cameras on this mast help navigate and provide stunning images.

Hubble Space Telescope (HST)
Launched in 1990, Hubble was the first jor optical telescope n space. It has taken amazing photos of the Universe.

The first ISS crew

| 1986 | 1990 | 2000 | 2005 | 2010 | 2012 | 2018 |

Mir Space Station
Mir was launched in 1986. Thirty-nine missions flew to it, up to June 2000.

SpaceX
The first private company to produce reusable rocket launchers and spacecraft.

Cassini-Huygens
Launched in 1997, it took over seven years to reach Saturn, exploring it until 2017.

Transiting Exoplanet Survey Satellite
TESS will cover the whole sky over two years, looking for planets orbiting other stars.

The Radio and Plasma Wave Spectrometer measured radio signals from Saturn.

Things to find out:

DK findout!

Space Travel

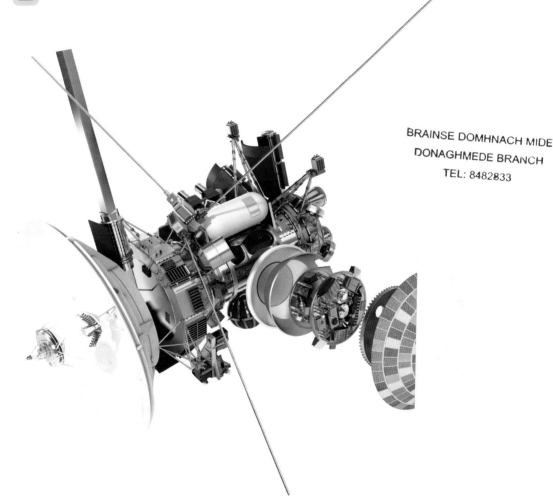

Author: Jerry Stone
Consultant: Peter Bond

DK | Penguin Random House

Senior editor Carrie Love
Editor Kritika Gupta
Designer Bettina Myklebust Stovne
Art editor Shubham Rohatgi
DTP designers Dheeraj Singh, Mohd Rizwan
Picture researcher Sakshi Saluja
Jacket co-ordinator Francesca Young
Jacket designer Suzena Sengupta
Managing editors Laura Gilbert, Monica Saigal
Deputy managing art editor Ivy Sengupta
Managing art editor Diane Peyton Jones
Senior producer, pre-production Tony Phipps
Senior producer Isabell Schart
Delhi team head Malavika Talukder
Creative director Helen Senior
Publishing director Sarah Larter
Educational consultant Jacqueline Harris

This book is dedicated to Phoebe

First published in Great Britain in 2019
by Dorling Kindersley Limited
80 Strand, London, WC2R 0RL

Copyright © 2019 Dorling Kindersley Limited
A Penguin Random House Company
10 9 8 7 6 5 4 3 2 1
001–311565–Feb/2019

A CIP catalogue record for this book
is available from the British Library.
ISBN: 978-0-2413-5839-9

Printed and bound in China.

A WORLD OF IDEAS:
SEE ALL THERE IS TO KNOW

www.dk.com

Contents

Chang'e 2

The Apollo 11 crew

Sojourner

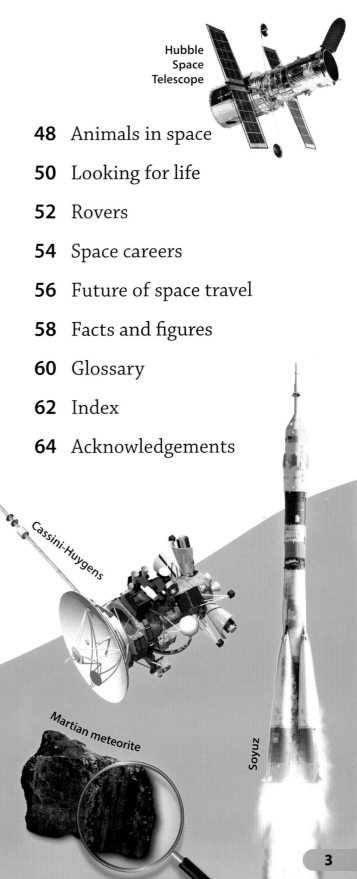

Hubble
Space
Telescope

Cassini-Huygens

Martian meteorite

Soyuz

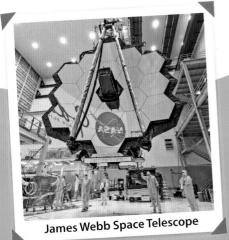

James Webb Space Telescope

What is space?

We live on planet Earth, one of eight main planets that orbit the Sun – our local star. Together with moons, rocky lumps called asteroids, and icy objects called comets, these make up our Solar System. The Solar System is part of a galaxy (a massive collection of stars) called the Milky Way. There may be about two trillion galaxies in the Universe.

Galaxies
Galaxies vary in size and shape. The galaxy shown here is a spiral galaxy, which spins around like a giant whirlpool.

What is in space?

Space contains all the planets, moons, stars, and galaxies, along with other things, such as star clusters (groups of stars) and nebulas (huge clouds of gas and dust). Space also contains dust, gas, and radiation.

The Cat's Paw and Lobster Nebulas

Stars and nebulas
Stars are giant shining globes of gas. There are about 250 billion stars in the Milky Way. In the two nebulas shown here, new stars are forming.

Why is space black?

To answer this, let's look at why our daytime sky is blue. This is because sunlight hits tiny things called molecules in the Earth's air and scatters them, causing the sky to look blue. In space, there is no air, so therefore it looks black.

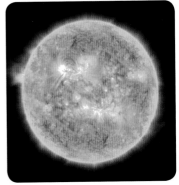

The Sun in space

Planets in space

Meteor shower

Planets and moons
We have eight main planets and five dwarf (small) planets in our Solar System. Most have one or more moons orbiting them.

Comets, asteroids, and meteors
There are millions of icy comets and rocky asteroids. Meteors are mainly tiny grains of dust.

Early astronomers

Astronomy is the study of space, including stars and planets. At first, people believed the Earth was at the centre of the Universe (the Geocentric system). Over time, people realized that planets orbited the Sun (the Heliocentric system). The invention of the telescope helped us understand the Universe better.

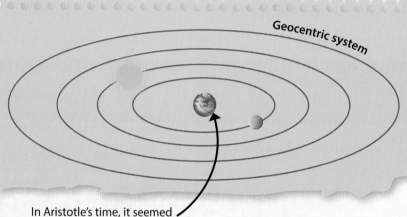

Geocentric system

In Aristotle's time, it seemed that the Sun, the Moon, and stars all circled the Earth.

Ptolemy
Living around 1,800 years ago, Ptolemy produced tables that could be used to predict the positions of the Sun, the Moon, and stars. He thought, incorrectly, that everything moved in perfect circles.

Aristotle
About 2,300 years ago, Aristotle believed the Earth was at the centre of everything. He thought that other objects revolved around the Earth, as this is what appeared to happen when watching them in the sky.

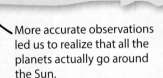

Heliocentric system

More accurate observations led us to realize that all the planets actually go around the Sun.

Copernicus

In 1543, Nicolaus Copernicus changed our view of the planets by suggesting that they all orbit the Sun. This went against the old idea that the Earth was the centre of everything.

Galileo made a refracting telescope, which means it used lenses. His early telescopes were much smaller than this one.

Galileo

After the telescope was invented in 1609, Italian scientist Galileo Galilei built one himself and observed the four main moons of Jupiter. Here were objects that clearly did not orbit the Earth. He also observed other objects, including the Sun and the Moon.

Space pioneers

The first human spaceflight was by Russian cosmonaut (astronaut) Yuri Gagarin in 1961. Since then, many other men and women have blazed a trail through space. Today, 12 April is celebrated around the world as "Yuri's Night", celebrating achievements in space exploration.

YURI GAGARIN

On 12 April 1961, Russian cosmonaut Yuri Gagarin made a single orbit around Earth in Vostok 1. This meant that the Soviet Union (Russia) had beaten its rival, the USA, with putting a human in space.

ALEXEI LEONOV

In 1965, Leonov became the first person to conduct an Extra Vehicular Activity (EVA) – a "spacewalk" – this is when astronauts go outside their spacecraft. Leonov spent 12 minutes outside Voshod 2.

THE APOLLO 11 CREW

Commander of Apollo 11, Neil Armstrong, was the first person in history to walk on the surface of another world. He landed the Lunar Module *Eagle* on the Moon with Edwin "Buzz" Aldrin on July 20, 1969. Michael Collins stayed in orbit around the Moon in the Command Module.

 **WOW!**

So far, around **550 people** have **flown** in space. Would **you** go?

VALENTINA TERESHKOVA

Two years after Gagarin's flight, Russia launched the first female cosmonaut in June 1963. She spent almost three days orbiting the Earth in Vostok 6. The next woman in space would not fly until 1982!

PEGGY WHITSON

Whitson holds the record for the most time spent in space by a woman, and by any American astronaut, at 665 days. In 2007, she became the first female commander of the ISS.

GENNADY PADALKA

The Russian cosmonaut Gennady Padalka made five spaceflights, one to the Russian space station Mir and four to the International Space Station (ISS). He holds the record for the most total time spent in space; 878 days.

The Space Race

The USA planned to launch a satellite into orbit around Earth in 1957. However, they were beaten by the launch of the Russian satellite, Sputnik 1, on 4 October 1957. The USA wanted to catch up, and so the Space Race between these two powerful nations was born.

Mercury 7
9 April 1959 – The USA announced its Project Mercury astronauts: (Back) Shepard, Grissom, Cooper; (Front) Schirra, Slayton, Glenn, and Carpenter.

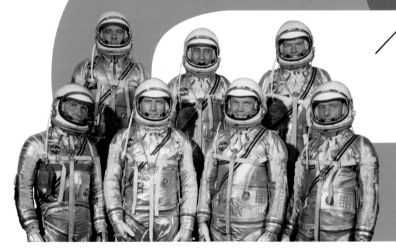

Kennedy's 1961 speech
25 May 1961 – President Kennedy challenged the USA to land a man on the Moon before the end of the decade.

First step on the Moon
Without any wind or rain on the Moon, the astronaut's footprints could last there for millions of years.

Man on the Moon
20 July 1969 – Neil Armstrong and Buzz Aldrin landed the Apollo 11 Lunar Module *Eagle*, and then walked on the Moon.

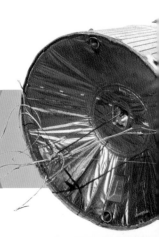

...tnik
...tober 1957 – Russia
...nched the first artificial
...llite, Sputnik 1. It circled
...Earth every 96 minutes.

The tiny Explorer 1
satellite weighed
14 kg (31 lb).

First American satellite
31 January 1958 – the USA's
first satellite, Explorer 1, led to the
discovery of the Van Allen radiation
belts. These trap high energy
solar particles.

The one man crew ejected and
parachuted back to Earth.

...ok 1
...April 1961 – Yuri Gagarin
...ame the first person in
...ce, making a single orbit
...e Earth in 108 minutes.

Lunar probe
6 October 1959 – Russia's
Luna 3 flew around the Moon,
taking photos of its far side –
the side not seen from Earth.

Luna 3's photos were picked up
by the radio telescope at Britain's
Jodrell Bank observatory.

In June 1965 Ed White made the
first American spacewalk.

First American in space
5 May 1961 – Alan Shepard
made a sub-orbital spaceflight,
and John Glenn flew into orbit
on 20 February 1962.

Project Gemini
Between March 1965 and December
1966, 10 two-man Gemini flights tried
out activities needed for the
Moon missions to follow.

Space programmes

Until recently, space programmes, or plans to explore, were carried out on behalf of government space agencies. Now private companies also run space activities, which will increase with the rise of space tourism (space travel for leisure). There are more than 70 national space agencies.

European Space Agency (ESA)
ESA launches satellites and space probes and also has a team of astronauts. Its headquarters are in Paris, France.

ESA's Gaia is a space observatory designed to produce the largest and most precise 3-D catalogue of space objects.

NASA's InSight was sent to Mars in 2018 to drill beneath its surface and study inside the planet.

National Aeronautics and Space Administration (NASA)
Created in 1958, NASA's projects inclu exploring the Solar System and beyo They also sent astronauts to the Moo

Russia's Mission Control space centre is in the city of Korolev.

Russian space agency (Roscosmos)
Formed in 1992 after the end of the Soviet Union, Roscosmos runs space activities for the Russian Federation.

China National Space Administration (CNSA)
Since 2003, China has sent more than 10 men and women into space. Chinese astronauts are called taikonauts.

In 2003, Yang Liwei became the first person sent into space by the Chinese space programme.

Chandrayaan-1 was India's first probe to the Moon. It was launched in 2008.

an Space Research
anisation (ISRO)
a has sent spacecraft
he Moon and to
s, and launched
ellites too.

The 37th launch of the very successful H-IIA rocket carried two satellites into orbit.

The Japan Aerospace Exploration Agency (JAXA)
Japan has launched space telescopes and probes for space research, communications, and observations.

Space Shuttle

From 1981 to 2011, the Space Shuttle was the United States' main space launch vehicle. Four Orbiters were originally built: *Columbia, Challenger, Discovery,* and *Atlantis. Columbia* and *Challenger* were destroyed in tragic accidents that killed their crews. *Endeavour* was built as a replacement for *Challenger.*

External Tank

The main engines were fuelled by the External Tank. This was separated after the engines were shut down. The tank broke up as it fell into the ocean.

Solid Rocket Boosters

Two Solid Rocket Boosters helped lift the Shuttle off the launch pad. They burned for two minutes, and then fell away, parachuting into the ocean, where they were picked up to be reused.

Orbiter

The Orbiter carried a crew of up to eight people, plus cargo. This was the only part that went into orbit. When it re-entered Earth's atmosphere, it glided to a runway

The Orbiters travelled a total of **872,906,379 km** (542,398,878 miles), carrying **355 different people.**

Discovery

United States

Main engines

The three main engines burned liquid hydrogen and liquid oxygen. Together, they produced nearly 540,000 kg (1.2 million lb) of thrust, taking the Orbiter from the ground to orbit in eight-and-a-half minutes.

Orbiter in space

Soon after lift-off, the boosters were dropped. The Orbiter's main engines continued for several more minutes. The External Tank was then discarded. Two smaller Orbital Maneuvering System (OMS) engines were used to get the Orbiter into orbit.

Visiting Mir
The Shuttle's missions to the Russian Mir space station paved the way for building the ISS.

2

The Orbiter
The crew and cargo travelled in the Orbiter.

Docking

Once in space, the Orbiter's cargo bay doors were opened to allow the docking system to connect to space stations such as Mir and the ISS.

1

Shuttle service

Unlike earlier spacecraft, NASA's Space Shuttle had reusable parts. Only the External Tank was lost. During its service life, the Shuttle was used to launch satellites, space telescopes, and probes. It also helped to assemble the International Space Station (ISS).

Lift-off!

Two Solid Rocket Boosters, the External Tank, and the Orbiter were mounted on a launch pad. The tank held fuel for the Orbiter's main engines during launch. The boosters gave extra power for lift-off.

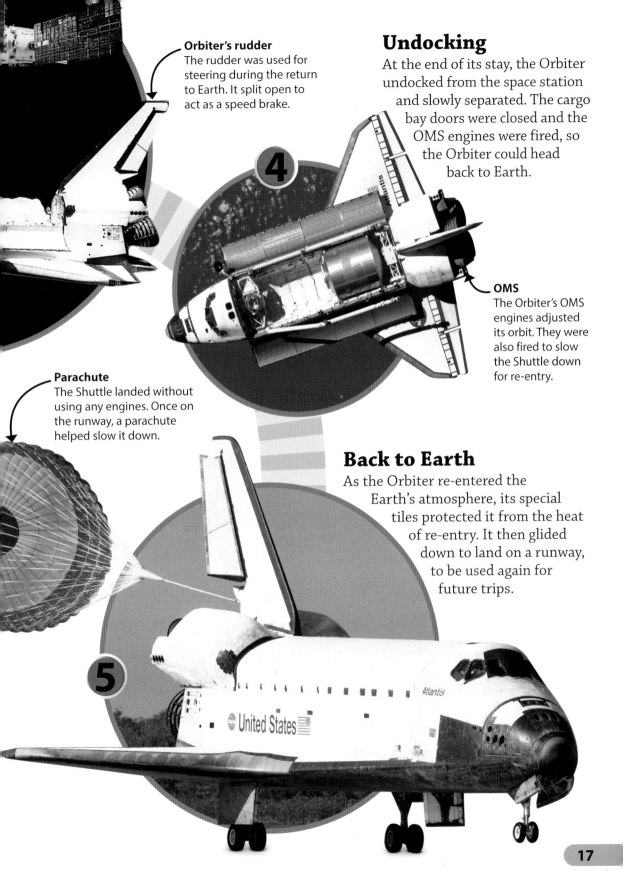

Orbiter's rudder
The rudder was used for steering during the return to Earth. It split open to act as a speed brake.

Undocking

At the end of its stay, the Orbiter undocked from the space station and slowly separated. The cargo bay doors were closed and the OMS engines were fired, so the Orbiter could head back to Earth.

4

OMS
The Orbiter's OMS engines adjusted its orbit. They were also fired to slow the Shuttle down for re-entry.

Parachute
The Shuttle landed without using any engines. Once on the runway, a parachute helped slow it down.

Back to Earth

As the Orbiter re-entered the Earth's atmosphere, its special tiles protected it from the heat of re-entry. It then glided down to land on a runway, to be used again for future trips.

5

United States

Atlantis

Rockets

A rocket is a vehicle – usually tube-shaped – with powerful engines that can blast it high into the sky. To reach orbit, rockets have more than one stage, or section. As each stage uses up its fuel, it is discarded. Some types of rocket made recently can be reused.

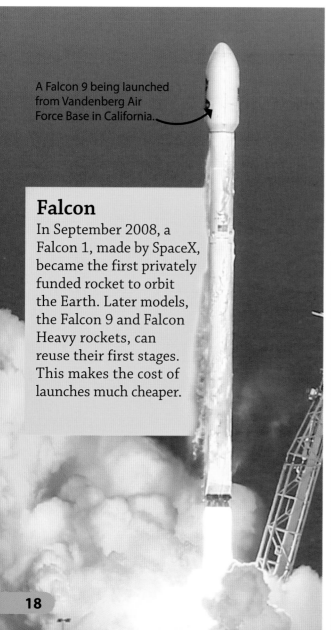

A Falcon 9 being launched from Vandenberg Air Force Base in California.

Falcon

In September 2008, a Falcon 1, made by SpaceX, became the first privately funded rocket to orbit the Earth. Later models, the Falcon 9 and Falcon Heavy rockets, can reuse their first stages. This makes the cost of launches much cheaper.

The Long March 2F was first launched in November 1999.

Long March 2F

This is the rocket that China has used to launch its two Tiangong space stations and the manned Shenzou spacecraft. It is a two-stage rocket, 62 m (203 ft) tall, and is launched from the Jiuquan Satellite Launch Center.

Saturn V rocket

The biggest and most powerful rocket ever to launch people into space was the Saturn V. It was 110 m (363 ft) high. Between December 1968 and December 1972, it carried Apollo astronauts to the Moon's orbit.

Saturn V rocket

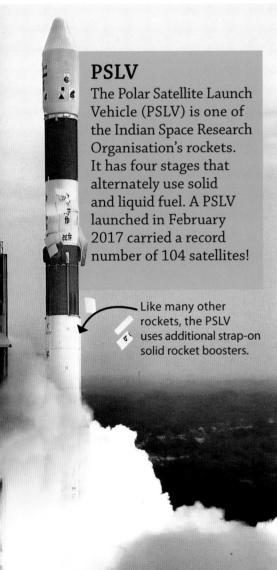

PSLV

The Polar Satellite Launch Vehicle (PSLV) is one of the Indian Space Research Organisation's rockets. It has four stages that alternately use solid and liquid fuel. A PSLV launched in February 2017 carried a record number of 104 satellites!

Like many other rockets, the PSLV uses additional strap-on solid rocket boosters.

The orbital module and descent module are in the top part of the spacecraft.

Soyuz

The Russian Soyuz spacecraft launches on a rocket of the same name. Since its first flight in 1966, it has become the most used and reliable launcher in the world, with more than 1,700 launches.

19

Spaceplanes

Unlike rockets that launch vertically, most spaceplanes take off horizontally. Spaceplanes all land horizontally on a runway, unlike spacecraft, such as Apollo. Spaceplanes can fly many times, which is one of their major features. A spaceflight is when a vehicle reaches space at a height of 100 km (62 miles) above sea level.

Eugen Sänger

Sänger was a spaceplane pioneer. Born in 1905, he came up with the idea of a craft that would be launched on a rocket sled and which could make sub-orbital flights. He also designed a two-part orbital spaceplane. His work greatly influenced later designs.

North American X-15

This is a rocket-powered aircraft carried by a B-52 bomber. Two flights by Joe Walker in July and August 1963 are spaceflights as they went above 100 km (62 miles).

SpaceShipOne

In 2004, SpaceShipOne made two spaceflights within two weeks, winning the $10 million (£7.5 million) Ansari X-Prize. SpaceShipOne was launched from a carrier aircraft and then fired its rocket motor.

Boeing X-37B

Launched vertically, the X-37B is an unmanned vehicle. It is operated by the United States Department of Defense. Full details of its space flights are not available to the public.

Skylon

Skylon is designed to be a spaceplane that can fly into orbit using an engine that first starts as a jet before working as a rocket. This will be possible due to the revolutionary SABRE engine.

Mach 1 is equivalent to the speed of sound. Mach 2 is twice the speed of sound, and so on. The X-15 holds the record for the fastest manned, powered aircraft at Mach 6.7, piloted by William Knight in 1967.

SpaceShipOne was carried by White Knight One. The larger SpaceShipTwo, carried by White Knight Two, is designed to carry up to six space tourists.

There are two X-37B craft, each carrying out long-duration missions of up to two years in orbit. They land automatically after returning from orbit.

Designed to operate unmanned, Skylon could carry 11 tonnes (12 tons) to the ISS – 45 per cent more than a reusable Falcon 9. Test flights could take place by 2025.

Mission Control

Spaceflights – both manned and unmanned – are controlled and monitored from a Mission Control Centre, where a team of people help run the flight. There are various centres around the world. The most famous one is at the Johnson Space Center in Houston, Texas, USA.

MISSION CONTROL CENTER

SPARTAN

ISO

OPS PLANNER

CAPCOM

SURGEON

KEY

1 **Display screens** Screens at the front of the room show the spacecraft's flight path, its status, and TV views from space.

2 **Flight Director** Responsible for control of the mission and for any actions needed for crew safety and mission success.

3 **Spacecraft communicator** An astronaut who provides all the voice communications between the ground and the spacecraft crew. Also called "CAPCOM", or capsule communicator.

4 **Extra Vehicular Activity (EVA) control** Responsible for all spacesuit and spacewalking-related tasks, equipment, and plans when there is EVA.

5 **Biomedical engineer (BME)** Provides 24-hour health-care support for the crew aboard the spacecraft.

6 **Flight surgeon** Monitors the crew's health, directs all the operational medical activities, and advises the Flight Director.

Mission to the Moon

People dreamed of flying to the Moon for many years. In the summer of 1969, just eight years after President Kennedy's challenge, Neil Armstrong and Edwin "Buzz" Aldrin became the first humans to walk on the Moon.

Apollo 11

On 20 July 1969, Armstrong and Aldrin landed their Lunar Module *Eagle*. Third crew member, Michael Collins, orbited the Moon overhead in the Command Module *Columbia*.

Armstrong and Aldrin explored the surface of the Moon for two-and-a-half hours.

Apollo 13 had to cancel landing on the Moon as there was an **emergency** on board.

Experiments were set up on the lunar surface while the Lunar Module was on the Moon.

Apollo missions

The Apollo 1 crew died in a fire during a launch rehearsal. Unmanned test flights paved the way for the other missions.

Apollo 7
In October 1968, Apollo 7 tested the redesigned spacecraft. The crew broadcast live TV images from space.

Apollo 8
The Apollo 8 crew was the first to fly to the Moon, making 10 lunar orbits, in December 1968.

Apollo 9
In March 1969, the crew of Apollo 9 tested the Lunar Module while in orbit around the Earth.

Apollo 10
This final rehearsal for a landing descended to within 16 km (10 miles) of the Moon's surface in May 1969.

Apollo 12
In November 1969, Apollo 12 landed close to the probe *Surveyor 3*, which had landed on the Moon in 1966.

Apollo 14
Alan Shepard was the only astronaut from Project Mercury to set foot on the Moon, in February 1971.

Apollo 15
This mission, in the summer of 1971, focused on science. Astronauts used an electric "Moon car" to explore.

Apollo 16
In April 1972, the Lunar Module landed in a highland region to study the Moon's much older rocks.

Apollo 17
The final landing, in December 1972, included the only geologist (rock expert) to visit the Moon.

The Apollo spacesuit

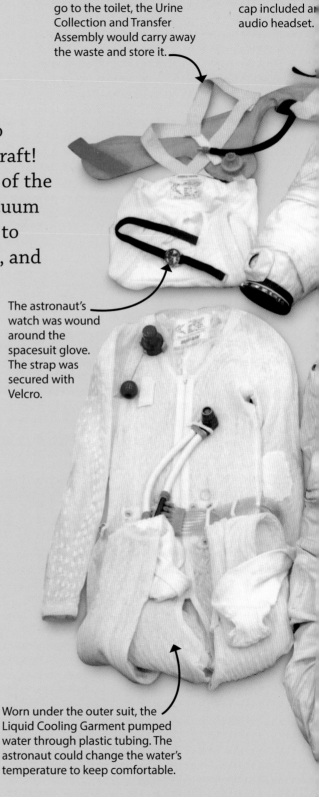

The spacesuit worn by the Apollo astronauts was a bit like a spacecraft! It gave protection from the glare of the Sun, tiny meteorites, and the vacuum of space. It also provided oxygen to breathe, removed carbon dioxide, and included a radio. Here is Neil Armstrong's spacesuit.

If an astronaut needed to go to the toilet, the Urine Collection and Transfer Assembly would carry away the waste and store it.

Communicatio cap included a audio headset.

The astronaut's watch was wound around the spacesuit glove. The strap was secured with Velcro.

Worn under the outer suit, the Liquid Cooling Garment pumped water through plastic tubing. The astronaut could change the water's temperature to keep comfortable.

Joseph Kosmo

Starting at NASA in 1961, Joseph Kosmo worked on the spacesuit for Project Mercury. He was also involved with the design and testing of spacesuits for Gemini, Apollo, Skylab, and the Space Shuttle before retiring in 2011.

Joseph Kosmo checks a spacesuit.

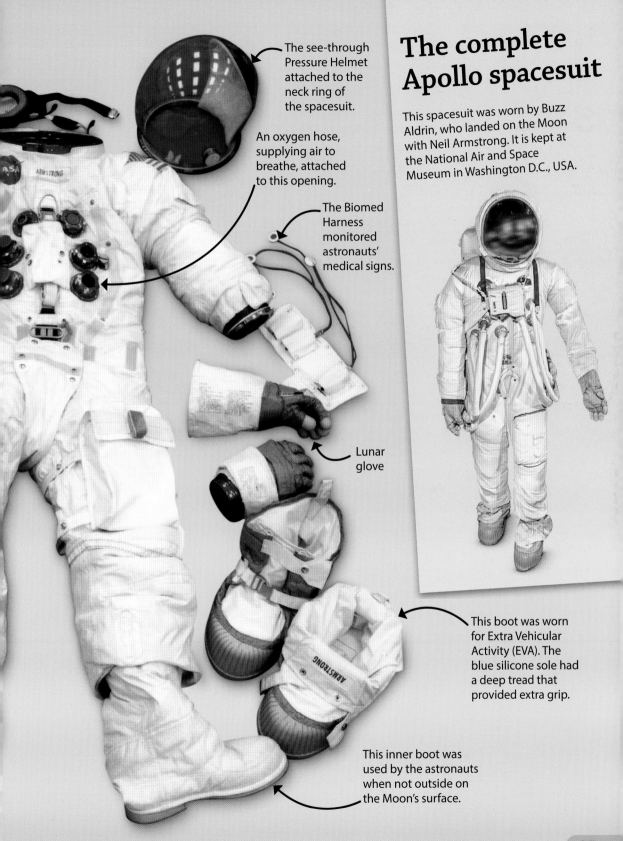

The see-through Pressure Helmet attached to the neck ring of the spacesuit.

An oxygen hose, supplying air to breathe, attached to this opening.

The Biomed Harness monitored astronauts' medical signs.

Lunar glove

The complete Apollo spacesuit

This spacesuit was worn by Buzz Aldrin, who landed on the Moon with Neil Armstrong. It is kept at the National Air and Space Museum in Washington D.C., USA.

This boot was worn for Extra Vehicular Activity (EVA). The blue silicone sole had a deep tread that provided extra grip.

This inner boot was used by the astronauts when not outside on the Moon's surface.

Space stations

A space station is a laboratory in space, where astronauts stay for long periods of time, carrying out scientific experiments. Large space stations are assembled in space, and other spacecraft dock onto them to deliver crews of astronauts and supplies.

International Space Station (ISS)

ISS crew members usually s[...] for expeditions of six mont[...] carrying out scientific resear[...] Living in weightlessness causes muscles to weaken, so astronauts must exercise[...] for two hours every day!

FACT FILE

» **Launched:** 29 September 2011

» **Current status:** Mission complete. Re-entered 2 April 2018

» **Length:** 10.5 m (34 ft)

» **Crew:** 2 crews of 3 astronauts

Tiangong-1

China launched Tiangong-1 ("Heavenly Palace") in 2011. It was visited by two crews in Shenzou spacecraft in 2012 and 2013. In 2018, after being shut down, the station burnt up re-entering the Earth's atmosphere.

The ISS has 16 main modules, which are powered by giant solar panels.

Mir

The Soviet Mir ("Peace") space station was visited by 28 crews: 104 different people from 12 different countries. Mir gave us a lot of valuable information on what it's like to live in space for long periods.

FACT FI[LE]

» **Launched:** 20 February 1986

» **Current status:** Mission complete. Re-entered 23 Mar[...] 2001

» **Length:** 31 m (1[...]

» **Crew:** 28 crews [...] cosmonauts

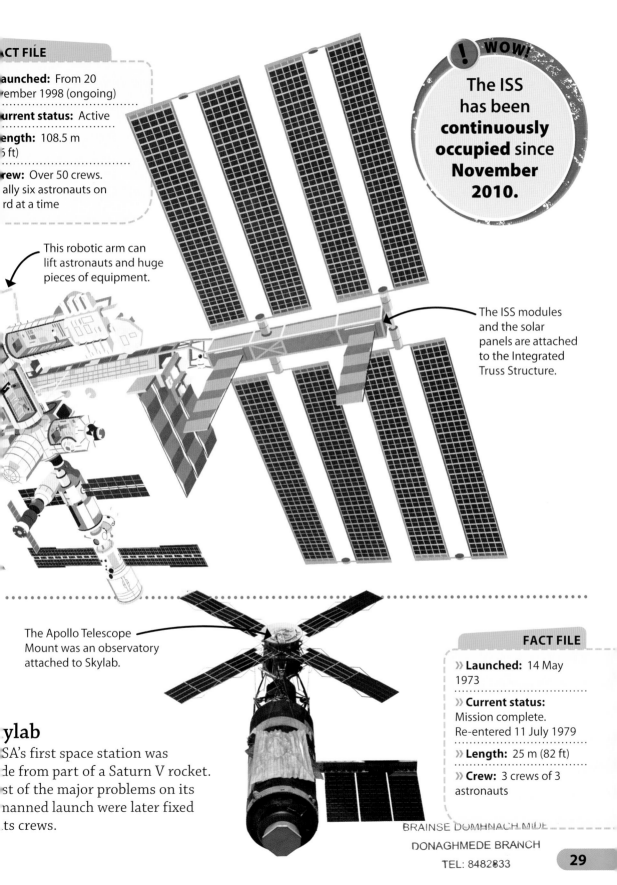

CT FILE

aunched: From 20
ember 1998 (ongoing)
....
urrent status: Active
....
ength: 108.5 m
ft)
....
rew: Over 50 crews.
ally six astronauts on
rd at a time

WOW!

The ISS
has been
**continuously
occupied** since
**November
2010.**

This robotic arm can
lift astronauts and huge
pieces of equipment.

The ISS modules
and the solar
panels are attached
to the Integrated
Truss Structure.

The Apollo Telescope
Mount was an observatory
attached to Skylab.

FACT FILE

>> **Launched:** 14 May
1973
....
>> **Current status:**
Mission complete.
Re-entered 11 July 1979
....
>> **Length:** 25 m (82 ft)
....
>> **Crew:** 3 crews of 3
astronauts

ylab

SA's first space station was
de from part of a Saturn V rocket.
st of the major problems on its
nanned launch were later fixed
ts crews.

Meet the expert

Dr Shannon Lucid became an astronaut in 1979, after completing the NASA training programme. She was the first woman to hold an international record for the most flight hours in orbit by any non-Russian. She retired from NASA in 2012.

Q: What inspired you as a child?

A: As a child I was intensely interested in the world around me. When I was in the fourth grade (Year 5) I somehow learned that water was composed of hydrogen and oxygen. To me this was the most amazing thing. How could two gases make a liquid? How could anyone find out something like this? I was told that it was found out by chemists, so right then and there I decided to become a chemist. Also, I read about inventor Robert Goddard and the rockets he was testing. I thought I could be a chemist and work with rockets.

Q: How did you become an astronaut?

A: I had wanted to explore space as a child, before there was even a space programme. Of course in the beginning of the human space programme in the US, was open only to males. As soon as NASA that they were going to hire more astronau including females, I applied and was accept

Q: How many hours did you spend in sp and how many missions did you go on i total?

A: I flew on five Space Shuttle missions fo total of 5,355 hours, or 223 days, in space

Q: What did lift-off into space feel like?

A: For me there was a great feeling of relief as soon as the solid rockets ignite because that meant we w going somewhere and li off would not be scrubb

Q: What was landing on Earth like?

A: The primary emotion had on re-entry and land was, "Oh my goodness, I so heavy! Do I really have live the rest of my life fee this heavy?"

First female astronauts
Shannon (second from the left) was among the first six women selected to be NASA astronauts.

What was a typical day like for you when you were in space?

I flew on both short duration Shuttle flights and a long duration flight of six months on the Russian space station Mir. The days on a short duration flight were very different from the days on a long duration flight. A short duration flight was like running a sprint race. You did not have to pace yourself, but put all your energy into getting to the finish line. A long duration flight is like a marathon. You have to pace yourself in order to be able to make it to the finish line.

What did it feel like to look down on Earth from space?

I spent as much free time as I could looking out the windows at the Earth. It always filled me with awe. I was impressed with how much of our Earth is water and as I flew over land masses, I also thought about how much of the Earth I had never travelled to!

Did you do any experiments in space?

Yes, I did many experiments in space. Many of the experiments were done to see how the human body changed in the space environment and how the human body adapted after returning to the Earth. I also did many experiments in physical science and biology.

Did you miss anything from Earth while you were living in space?

Of course I missed my family.

On Mir, I also missed sunshine on my face and the wind in my hair.

Q: What was the best thing about being an astronaut?

A: The best thing about being an astronaut and flying in space was the people that you worked with.

Q: What was the worst thing about being an astronaut?

A: The worst thing about being an astronaut was the long wait to be assigned to a flight.

Q: What would your advice for a future astronaut be?

A: My advice is to study what you are really interested in and not to second-guess what will be criteria for getting hired as an astronaut, because things change. Just do the best that you can!

Shannon relaxing during her off-duty time in the Shuttle Spacehab module.

Living in space

People and objects – if not tied down – float in space. This state, called microgravity, makes things appear to be weightless. It creates daily life challenges for astronauts. Here are some of the experiences they have to deal with during their time in space.

Cleaning up

Water floats around in balls in space. To keep clean, astronauts use flannels and sponges. When washing hair, they use no-rinse shampoo.

Keeping fit

In space, muscles and bones can weaken. To prevent this from happening, astronauts need to do two hours of exercise every day.

Food

Food tastes different in space. Meals come in sealed packages and often need water added. Astronauts look forward to supplies of fresh fruit.

Nom! Nom! Nom!

Working

The ISS is a microgravity research laboratory. Most of the astronauts' work involves various kinds of science. The results help us on Earth.

Spacewalk

Sometimes astronauts go outside to install new equipment, fit new sections onto the space station, or carry out repairs. This work can take many hours.

Fun and games

In their time off, astronauts can play musical instruments and read books. However, what they enjoy most is looking out of the windows at the Earth down below.

Talking to loved ones

Astronauts have always been able to talk with their families by radio. The ISS has internet, and the astronauts can use email.

Sleeping

Astronauts use sleeping bags. To stop themselves from floating around – and bumping into things – when asleep, they can attach themselves to a wall.

Experiments in space

Experiments done in space help us learn not only about the Earth and space, but also how the human body is affected by being in space. This is vital if we want to travel to other planets, such as Mars.

Microbes were tested on the ISS, rather than being brought back to the Earth to be looked at. This was a scientific first!

Microbes
Microbes are tiny organisms, many of which are vital to human health. However, others can cause disease. In 2017, astronauts took samples of microbes found on the outside of the ISS! Luckily, they found all the samples to be harmless.

WOW!

In 2014, **48** types of **microbes** from Earth were sent to the **ISS** to see how they **behave in space.**

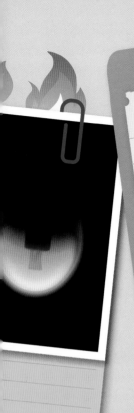

Studying motion sickness

On a Spacelab mission flown on the Space Shuttle in 1996, astronauts carried out more than 40 experiments. In the Torso Rotation Experiment, Canadian astronaut Bob Thirsk studied the causes of motion sickness and ways in which to prevent it.

Bob Thirsk during the Torso Rotation Experiment.

These red lettuces were grown on the ISS.

Growing food

Growing food in space will be essential in the future for long flights to places such as Mars. Fresh food can provide vitamins, and it reduces the need for packaged food. Astronauts on the ISS have eaten lettuce grown in space.

Space lab

China launched Tiangong-2 ("Heavenly Palace"), a space laboratory, in September 2016. Two astronauts were on board the space lab for 30 days. They carried out scientific and technical tests on the effects of weightlessness on the human body.

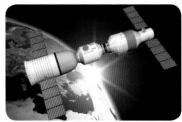

A Shenzou spacecraft docked to a Tiangong space station.

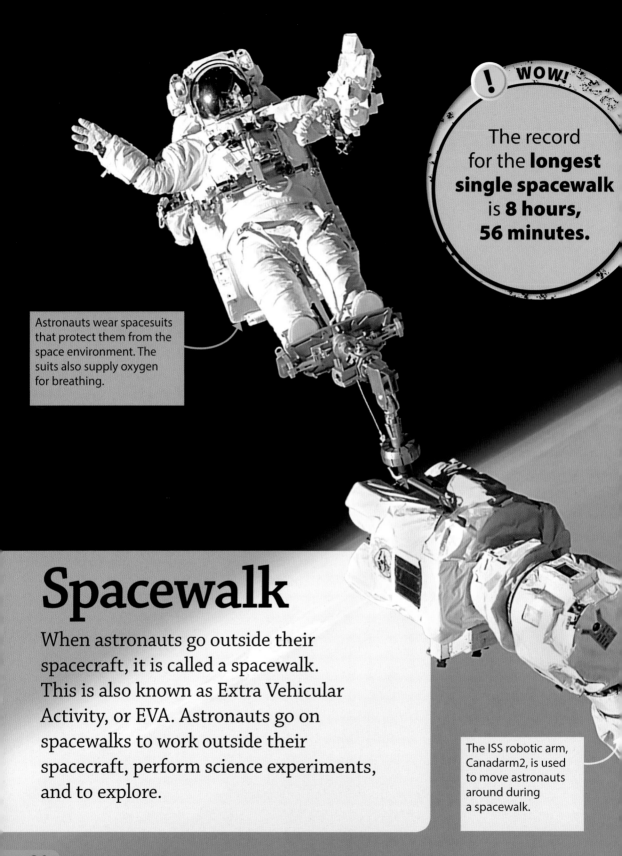

The record for the **longest single spacewalk** is **8 hours, 56 minutes.**

Astronauts wear spacesuits that protect them from the space environment. The suits also supply oxygen for breathing.

Spacewalk

When astronauts go outside their spacecraft, it is called a spacewalk. This is also known as Extra Vehicular Activity, or EVA. Astronauts go on spacewalks to work outside their spacecraft, perform science experiments, and to explore.

The ISS robotic arm, Canadarm2, is used to move astronauts around during a spacewalk.

Training for spacewalks

Before each mission, astronauts train for the job they need to perform in space. They spend hours learning how to handle space equipment.

Astronauts prepare for spacewalks by training underwater in a giant pool. By floating in water, astronauts feel like they are floating in space.

Virtual reality equipment is used to practise spacewalks. Astronauts wear a helmet with a video screen inside. It makes the astronauts feel as if they are really in space!

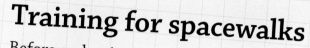

Training is carried out in the Partial Gravity Simulator (POGO) test area. Here, astronauts feel what it is like to move under gravity that is lower than that on Earth.

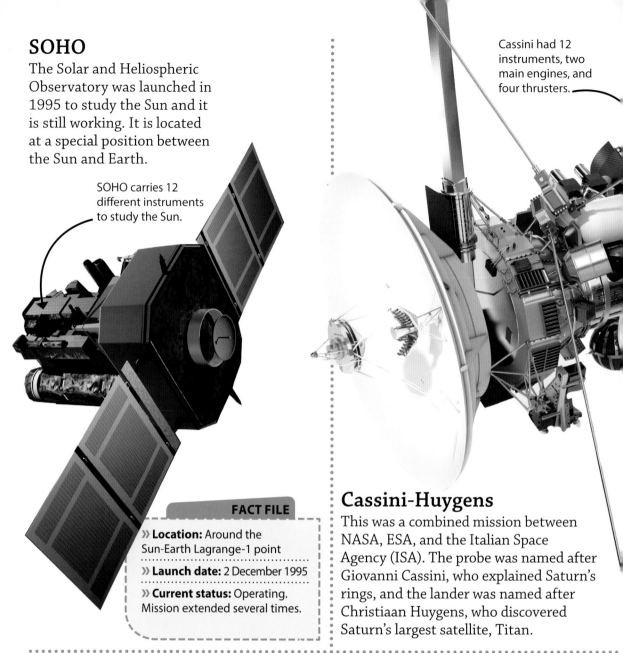

SOHO

The Solar and Heliospheric Observatory was launched in 1995 to study the Sun and it is still working. It is located at a special position between the Sun and Earth.

SOHO carries 12 different instruments to study the Sun.

Cassini had 12 instruments, two main engines, and four thrusters.

FACT FILE

» **Location:** Around the Sun-Earth Lagrange-1 point

» **Launch date:** 2 December 1995

» **Current status:** Operating. Mission extended several times.

Cassini-Huygens

This was a combined mission between NASA, ESA, and the Italian Space Agency (ISA). The probe was named after Giovanni Cassini, who explained Saturn's rings, and the lander was named after Christiaan Huygens, who discovered Saturn's largest satellite, Titan.

Searching space

Since Luna 1 in 1959, we have sent a wide range of unmanned spacecraft to investigate the Moon, the Sun, and the planets, as well as asteroids and comets. They have helped us learn far more than we could from ground instruments.

The Huygens probe became the first craft to land on Titan.

The 2.7 m (9 ft) heat-shield protected Huygens during entry through Titan's atmosphere.

Rosetta contained science instruments and a high-resolution camera.

Rosetta

A European Space Agency mission to study comet 67P/Churyumov-Gerasimenko, it became the first craft to orbit a comet, and the Philae lander was the first craft to land on one.

FACT FILE

» **Destination:** Comet 67P/Churyumov-Gerasimenko

» **Launch date:** 2 March 2004

» **Current status:** De-orbited 30 September 2016

New Horizons

This was the first spacecraft ever sent to Pluto. After its flyby in 2015, it was re-targeted to fly past object 2014 MU69, in the Kuiper Belt region, in January 2019.

FACT FILE

» **Destination:** 1) Pluto 2) 2014-MU69, "Ultima Thule"

» **Launch date:** 19 January 2006

» **Current status:** In the Kuiper Belt

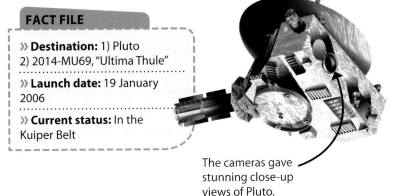

The cameras gave stunning close-up views of Pluto.

FACT FILE

Destination: The Moon, and asteroid 4179 Toutatis

Launch date: 1 October 2010

Current status: It completed work in lunar orbit and then went on to explore interplanetary space.

Chang'e 2

A follow on from China's Chang'e 1 lunar probe, it carried out research to help prepare for Chang'e 3's lander and lunar rover in 2013.

Chang'e 2 took lots of high quality images of the Moon and the asteroid Toutatis.

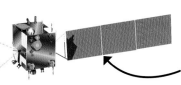

Space telescopes

Telescopes in space allow us to see more of the Universe than telescopes on the Earth. That's because the Earth's atmosphere blocks out a lot of the radiation, including gamma rays, X-rays, ultraviolet, infrared, and radio waves, given off by stars and other distant objects.

CHANDRA X-RAY OBSERVATORY

Named after the astrophysicist Subrahmanyan Chandrasekhar, this telescope was launched in 1999 from the Space Shuttle. It is much better at detecting X-ray sources than earlier telescopes.

Spektr-R

Launched in 2011, Spektr-R is a radio telescope with a 10 m (33 ft) diameter antenna. By working together with observatories on the Earth, it can obtain extremely high levels of detail not possible before.

KEPLER MISSION

This telescope focuses on a small area of our galaxy. It measures changes in starlight to detect planets orbiting other stars. So far it has found more than 2,000 planets.

HUBBLE SPACE TELESCOPE

Hubble is named after the astronomer Edwin Hubble. It has given us many amazing pictures of the Universe since its launch in 1990. Hubble orbits the Earth at a speed of 27,350 kph (17,000 mph).

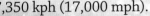

SPITZER SPACE TELESCOPE

This telescope was named after astronomer Lyman Spitzer, who, in 1946, suggested putting telescopes in space. It was launched in 2003, and detects infrared, or heat radiation, given off by objects in space.

Fermi gamma-ray space telescope

Launched in 2008, this telescope searches all directions for explosions of light, called gamma-ray bursts, in distant galaxies; other high-energy sources; and evidence of dark matter.

! WOW!

The massive **James Webb Space Telescope (JWST)** is due to be launched in **2021**.

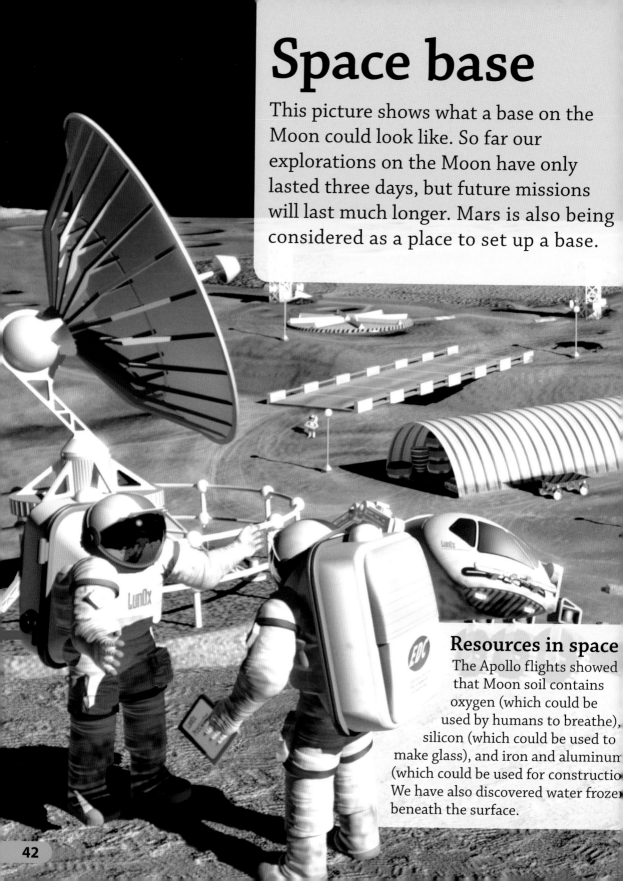

Space base

This picture shows what a base on the Moon could look like. So far our explorations on the Moon have only lasted three days, but future missions will last much longer. Mars is also being considered as a place to set up a base.

Resources in space

The Apollo flights showed that Moon soil contains oxygen (which could be used by humans to breathe), silicon (which could be used to make glass), and iron and aluminum (which could be used for construction We have also discovered water froze beneath the surface.

Space shelters

Humans wanting to live on the Moon or Mars will have to learn to live with the harsh conditions, such as low temperatures and thin air.

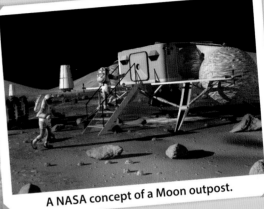

A NASA concept of a Moon outpost.

Lunar outpost
When we return to the Moon in the future, astronauts might use a shelter like this whilst exploring during a couple of weeks on the surface.

Astronauts on Mars might bury their habitats with local soil.

Martian habitats
On the Moon and Mars, people need protection from radiation (such as X-rays and high energy particles). One way could be to cover the habitats with soil, which would also shelter people from extreme temperatures.

Exploring space

We explore space in many ways. We have unmanned craft such as satellites, space probes, and space telescopes. We also have manned spacecraft, and have been to the Moon.

Roll a die and begin exploring.

START

Are you ready for your space quest?

Find out about some of our amazing achievements in space exploration by playing this board game.

9

Viking 1

8

1 You are working on a rocket to take you to the Moon. Miss a turn!

7 Oh no! Your probe crashed. Go back one space!

2

Saturn V

TESS

The Transiting Exoplanet Survey Satellite (TESS) is a space telescope designed to search for exoplanets. These are planets outside of the Solar System. At the time of launch in 2018, fewer than 4,000 exoplanets had been found – TESS is expected to discover over 20,000.

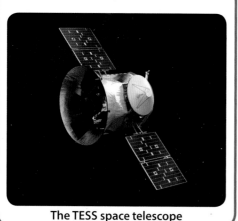

The TESS space telescope

3 The first humans have landed on the Moon! Move ahead 3 spaces.
Apollo 11 astronauts, Neil Armstrong and Buzz Aldrin landed on the Moon while Michael Collins orbited the Moon, on 20 July 1969.

6

Marine

5 The first pictures Mercury are taken Roll the dice again.
Space probe Mariner was able to map abou 45 per cent of Mercury surface before its fina flyby on 16 March 197

4

0 First Mars landing! Move ahead one space.
...ng 1 became the ... spacecraft to ...cessfully land on ...rs on 20 July 1976.

11

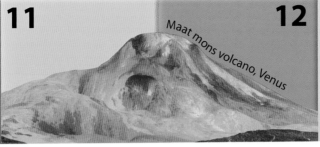

Maat mons volcano, Venus

12

13 Your lander transmitted coloured pictures! Move ahead 2 spaces.
Venera 13 landed on 1 March 1982. It was the first lander to transmit colour images from the surface of Venus.

17 Your probe uncovered ...une's secrets. ...e ahead 2 spaces.
...s flyby of Neptune in ..., Voyager 2 confirmed ...ings and six ...own moons.

16 Your probe discovered new moons! Roll the die again.
Voyager 2 discovered 11 moons when it reached Uranus in 1986!

15

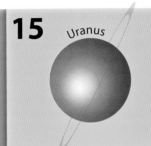

Uranus

14 You lost communication. Miss a turn and work on your probe!

8 Your probe has launched ...ander! Move ...d 1 space.
...ni's lander Huygens ...ended onto Saturn's ...n Titan in 2005.

19

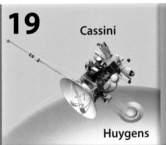

Cassini

Huygens

20 Your probe crashed into a small asteroid. You'll have to build it again. Move back 3 spaces and miss a turn!

21

25

...ew Horizons

24 You've reached Pluto! Roll the die again.
New Horizons spacecraft was the first ever to visit dwarf planet Pluto in July 2015.

23

Juno

Your spacecraft has entered Jupiter's orbit! Move ahead 1 space. **22**
NASA's spacecraft Juno entered orbit around Jupiter on 5 July 2016.

6 Successful landing on a comet! Move ...ad 2 spaces.
...etta spacecraft's ...der module Philae, ...cessfully landed ...a comet on ... November 2014.

27

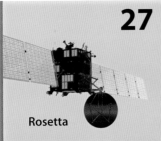

Rosetta

Congratulations! You've finished your voyage.
However, our exploration of space continues. Spacecraft are launched all the time, and we are planning to return to the Moon and go to Mars!

FINISH

Space tourism

In 2001, Dennis Tito became the first "spaceflight participant", or space tourist. Before then only astronauts and cosmonauts had flown into space, sent by the country they came from. Tito paid more than £15 million (US $20 million) to spend a week on the ISS. He had to complete training before heading into space.

KEY

1 **Virgin Galactic** SpaceShipTwo will be released from a carrier aircraft, and then fire a rocket engine to reach space.

2 **Blue Origin** Started by the founder of Amazon, Jeff Bezos, Blue Origin is developing reusable spacecraft and launchers.

3 **ISS** This is currently the only place in orbit where people can stay. There are plans for space hotels.

4 **Space junk** One problem facing satellites and spacecraft is the amount of waste orbiting the Earth, from flecks of paint to leftover rocket stages. Hitting even a tiny item at high speeds can cause serious damage!

Virgin Galactic will fly its passengers to over 100 km (62 miles), giving them six minutes of weightlessness.

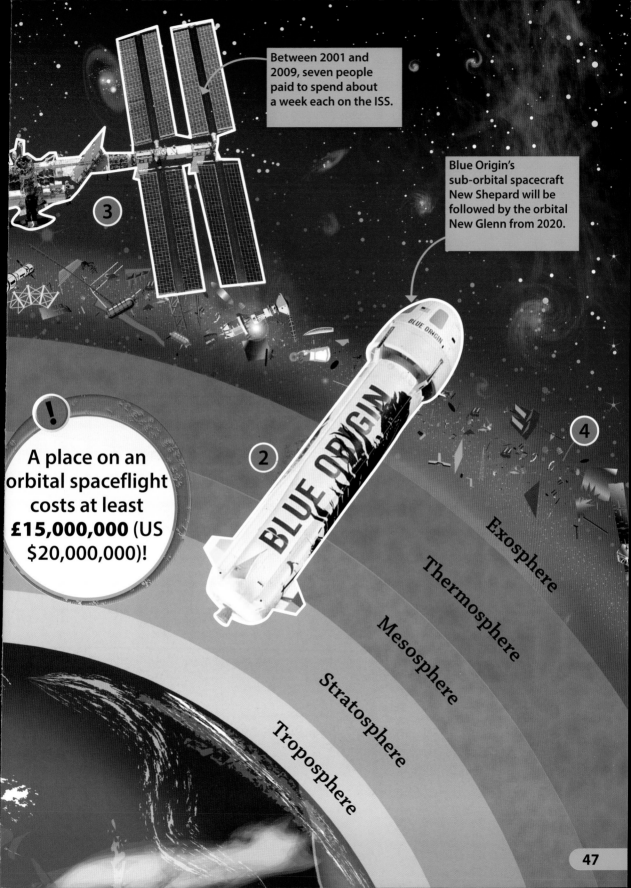

Between 2001 and 2009, seven people paid to spend about a week each on the ISS.

3

Blue Origin's sub-orbital spacecraft New Shepard will be followed by the orbital New Glenn from 2020.

4

2

A place on an orbital spaceflight costs at least **£15,000,000** (US **$20,000,000**)!

BLUE ORIGIN

Exosphere

Thermosphere

Mesosphere

Stratosphere

Troposphere

Fruit fly

The first animals in space were fruit flies launched in 1947 by the United States on a captured German V2 rocket. They were ejected and recovered.

REALLY?

In 1968, Russia sent **two tortoises** around the Moon on **Zond 5.**

Mouse

The first space mouse was launched in 1950 on a V2 rocket. In June 2018, SpaceX launched 20 mice to the ISS.

Dog

In 1957, Russia launched the first living creature to orbit the Earth, a dog named Laika ("Barker"), but the spacecraft could not be recovered.

In 1973, two spiders, Anita and Arabella, were taken to the Skylab space station to see if they could spin a web when weightless – they could!

Tardigrade

In 2007, the European Space Agency's (ESA) FOTON-M3 mission carried some tardigrades, also known as water bears, which survived 10 days of exposure to open space.

Animals in space

Before humans went into space, Russia and the United States sent animals to see if space was safe for people. Russia used dogs; the United States used chimpanzees. All kinds of animals have been flown into space, including newts, fish, frogs, rabbits, shrimp, and cats.

Looking for life

One of our biggest questions as humans is, "Are we alone?". Is Earth the only planet in the Universe that has life? We have found thousands of planets around other stars, and research suggests that many should have life, but we cannot tell for sure.

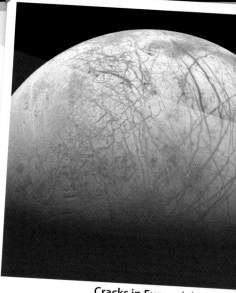
Cracks in Europa's ice

Europa

One of the four main moons of Jupiter, Europa has a very smooth surface of ice. There could be liquid water below, which makes it possible that life could exist there.

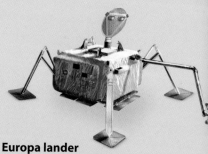

Europa lander
This is a lander that could search for life on Europa. It would need to drill through ice into the ocean to find anything!

Mars today is a desert world

Life on Mars?

We have learned that Mars used to be warmer and wetter than it is now, so it might be possible that it had life in the past.

Meteorite
This meteorite was thought to contain bacteria from Mars. Scientists are not sure.

Green Bank Telescope

This is the world's largest fully-steerable radio telescope. Since 2016, it has been part of the "Breakthrough Listen project", which is expected to last 10 years. It is searching for possible signals from other worlds.

The GBT in West Virginia, USA

The Arecibo Observatory in Puerto Rico

The Arecibo Signal

In 1974, the Arecibo Observatory telescope was upgraded, and the staff sent a message out into the Universe. A receiver can decode it and produce the diagram shown here.

The decoded message
It was sent in binary code. Colours have been added to make sections stand out.

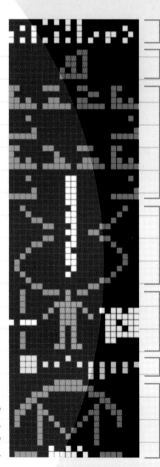

Number 1–10 (White).

Atomic numbers for hydrogen, carbon, nitrogen, oxygen, and phosphorus (Purple).

Chemical components of DNA (Green).

Information on human DNA (White) and a diagram of the double-helix (Blue).

A human figure, (Red). Average height (Blue/White).

Human population (White).

The Solar System, indicating the Earth (Yellow).

The Arecibo radio telescope (Purple). Size of telescope (Blue/White).

Rovers

Rovers are vehicles designed to travel across the surface of a planet or moon. They can operate for longer than astronauts, and in places that could be dangerous for humans, but they need to be programmed and cannot be repaired.

Lunokhod 1 and

The Soviet Union's Lunokhod 1 only drove 10.54 km (6.5 miles) over 321 days (11 lunar days), but Lunokhod 2 lasted fo four months, covering 39 km (24.2 miles).

Lunokhod's tracks on the lunar surface.

The astronauts are over 5 km (3.1 miles) away from the Lunar Module.

Lunar Roving Vehicle

The last three Apollo missions each carried a Lunar Roving Vehicle (LRV) – an electric car. They let the astronauts travel across the Moon, exploring a large area and gathering a wider range of samples.

The LRVs were powered by two batteries.

FACT FILE

» **Landed:** 4 July 1997

» **Destination:** Ares Vallis, Mars

» **Mission status:** Completed 27 September 1997

Sojourner's view towards the Twin Peaks on Mars.

Sojourner was just 55 cm (25.5 in) long.

Sojourner

NASA's Mars Pathfinder carried a small rover, called Sojourner. Although it only explored Mars for three months, travelling just 100 m (328 ft), it showed that it was possible to use a rover on Mars. Later rovers were much larger.

View of the base of Mount Sharp.

FACT FILE

» **Landed:** 6 August 2012

» **Destination:** Gale Crater, Mars

» **Mission status:** Ongoing

Its robotic arm holds five instruments.

Curiosity

NASA's fourth Mars rover, the Mars Science Laboratory, known as Curiosity. It's the size of a small car and is nuclear-powered, unlike previous craft that relied on solar panels to charge batteries.

Spacecraft or rocket engineer

These people design and build satellites, space probes, planetary rovers, and manned spacecraft. They make all the parts and then assemble them.

Science officer

The ISS is a science laboratory. You could design experiments, and even carry them out on board.

Space careers

What happens in space affects almost all of us on a daily basis, such as weather forecasting, satellite navigation (Sat Nav) systems in cars, satellite TV, and much more. Apart from working in space, there are all kinds of space-related careers that you could do. The jobs all have different locations.

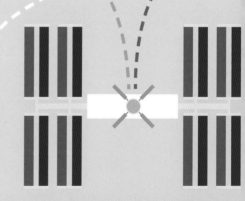

Mission Control centre
This is where spaceflights are managed and monitored, usually all the way from lift-off to landing. One of the many jobs based here is that of a flight controller.

ISS
Thousands of people have jobs linked with the ISS. There are astronauts living and working on board the ISS, but there are also people on the Earth doing a variety of jobs that support these astronauts.

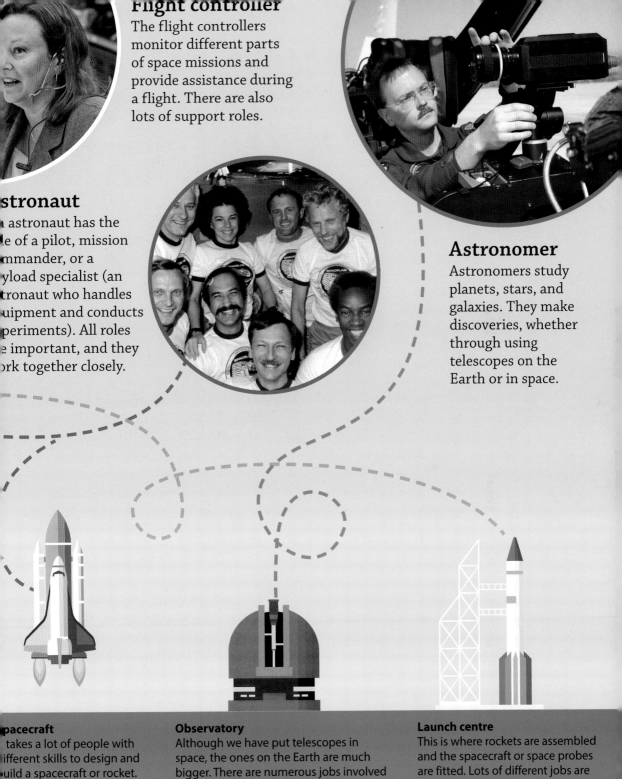

Flight controller

The flight controllers monitor different parts of space missions and provide assistance during a flight. There are also lots of support roles.

Astronaut

An astronaut has the role of a pilot, mission commander, or a payload specialist (an astronaut who handles equipment and conducts experiments). All roles are important, and they work together closely.

Astronomer

Astronomers study planets, stars, and galaxies. They make discoveries, whether through using telescopes on the Earth or in space.

Spacecraft
It takes a lot of people with different skills to design and build a spacecraft or rocket.

Observatory
Although we have put telescopes in space, the ones on the Earth are much bigger. There are numerous jobs involved in the running of an observatory.

Launch centre
This is where rockets are assembled and the spacecraft or space probes are fitted. Lots of different jobs are needed for lift-off!

Future of space travel

In the immediate future, humans will continue to work on the ISS. Plans are in place to send astronauts back to the Moon and then on to Mars. Unmanned craft will continue to explore the Solar System and look out to the rest of the Universe. There is so much we've yet to discover.

Planned missions

OSIRIS-Rex is a NASA mission launched in 2016. It's due to bring back samples from an asteroid in 2023. NASA sent InSight in 2018. It is heading to Mars to drill below the ground. ESA and NASA will launch craft to Mars in 2020.

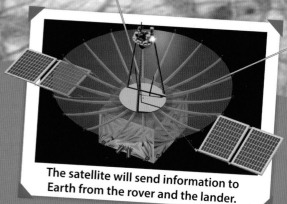

The satellite will send information to Earth from the rover and the lander.

Chang'e 4
Chang'e 4 was planned as the first craft to land on the far side of the Moon. A separate communications satellite will relay signals from the lander.

Humans in space

In 2021, ESA and NASA are due to launch up to four astronauts in a manned Orion mission. This will be the first time humans have left low orbit since 1972. Virgin Galactic plans to fly hundreds of space tourists, and Elon Musk (the founder of SpaceX) wants to send large numbers of people to the Moon and to Mars.

The ESA-NASA Orion spacecraft

Europa probe
Jupiter's moon, Europa, is covered in ice. It may have a liquid water ocean underneath, where life might exist.

Its huge mirror is five times as big as Hubble's.

Robonaut 2 does dangerous EVA jobs in place of an astronaut.

James Webb Space Telescope (JWST)
A successor to the Hubble Space Telescope (HST), JWST will operate in infra-red wavelengths, allowing it to detect objects too old and distant for Hubble to observe.

Robotic explorers
Robonaut 2 is being tested on the ISS, and full robotic explorers may help us explore space, going to distant places and locations too dangerous for humans.

Facts and figures

Space is filled with unknown things and many surprises. Here are some weird and wonderful facts about space and space travel that you can impress your friends with.

Scientists believe that **HUMANS** could actually be **exploring Mars** by **2040**.

HUMANS have been **travelling** into space since **1961**.

127

127 kg

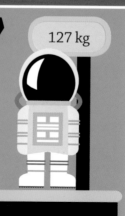

A spacesuit weighs approximately 127 kg (280 lb) – without the astronaut. It takes between 30–45 minutes to put it on.

400

We've been using telescopes for more than 400 years to look into space.

The total cost of the entire Apollo programme was **£19 billion (US $25.4 billion)**. In today's money, that's around **£112 billion (US $150 billion)**.

Bruce McCandless was the first astronaut to float untethered from a spacecraft during an EVA.

In **2001**, a pizza company **"DELIVERED"a pizza** by rocket **to astronauts** on board the ISS.

50

here are about 0 launch sites round the Earth.

1,000

To become a pilot-astronaut, the candidate must have completed 1,000 hours of flying time in a jet aircraft.

Glossary

Here are explanations of a number of words to do with space travel.

Arecibo message Radio message broadcast into space by the Arecibo Observatory giving information about humans and the Earth, in the hope it might reach intelligent alien life

asteroid Rocky object smaller than a planet. Most asteroids orbit the Sun, between Mars and Jupiter

astronaut Space traveller; someone who is trained to take part in a spaceflight

astrophysicist Someone who studies the nature of stars and galaxies

atmosphere Layers of gases surrounding a planet, moon, or star

comet Icy object orbiting a star. When it gets closer to the star, a tail may form

dark matter Invisible material believed to exist in space. Astrophysicists think that dark matter makes up 80 per cent of material in the Universe

dwarf planet Any of five objects, including Pluto, in our Solar System that are smaller than the eight main planets

Earth Third planet from the Sun. The home of the human race and where all known life exists

galaxy Huge collection of stars, from a few hundred million up to thousands of billions of stars

gravity Force that causes all things to be attracted to others. It explains why apples fall to the ground and why planets orbit the Sun

infrared Radiation with wavelengths longer than that of visible light. Infrared astronomy can show objects from the early period of the Universe

laboratory Place where scientific experiments are carried out

lunar Belonging to the M...

Mars Fourth planet from the Sun and target of man... spacecraft as part of our search for life elsewhere

matter In general terms, anything that has mass an... takes up some space

meteor Object that burns... when passing at high spee... through the atmosphere. Usually about the size of a grain of sand, meteors are known as "shooting stars"

Milky Way Spiral galaxy t... contains our Solar System

module Unit of a spacecra...

moon Natural satellite of... a planet

nebula Cloud of gas and d... in space

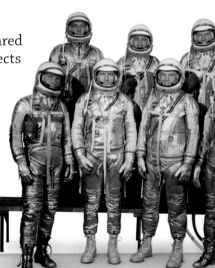

The Project
Mercury astronauts

it Path of an object
und another, such as
anet around a star

iter Part of the Space
ttle that carried cargo
crew members into orbit

net Round object, such
Mars, Venus, or Jupiter,
t orbits the Sun

be Unmanned spacecraft
igned to study objects in
ce and send information
k to the Earth

er Wheeled vehicle,
er manned or unmanned,
d to explore the surface
planet or other body

ellite Object that
its another body, such
planet around a star
spacecraft around
Earth

ar Belonging to the Sun

ar System Sun and the
er objects that orbit it

ce Also known as
ter space", the region
ond the Earth's
osphere between
er objects

cecraft Vehicle, either
nned or unmanned,
igned to fly in space

spaceflight Voyage by
a spacecraft into space
above the Earth or deeper
into space

Space Race Rival
space-related activities
between the Soviet Union
and the United States. It
started with the launch of
Sputnik 1 and resulted in the
first humans on the Moon

spaceplane Vehicle designed
to be launched into space and
land on a runway, to be reused

space probe Spacecraft that
does not orbit the Earth but
is sent to explore deep space
or other planets

Space Shuttle General term
for the Space Transportation
System, consisting of the
Space Shuttle Orbiter, its
Solid Rocket Boosters, and
External Tank

spacesuit Protective clothing
worn by space travellers to
provide oxygen, a radio, and
protection from the
environment of space

spacewalk Also called Extra
Vehicular Activity (EVA), any
activity in which an astronaut
goes outside a spacecraft,
such as to make repairs or
walk on the Moon's surface

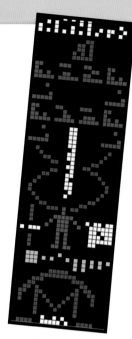

Arecibo message

stage Section of a rocket

star Huge ball of gas
generating light and heat

Sun Star at the centre
of our Solar System. The
Earth and other planets
orbit the Sun

telescope Instrument for
looking at distant objects

ultraviolet Radiation with
wavelengths shorter than
that of visible light

Universe Everything in
space, including all the stars,
nebulae, and galaxies

weightlessness Lack of
weight in space that allows
people and objects to float

Index

Acknowledgements

The publisher would like to thank the following people for their assistance in the preparation of this book: Caroline Bingham, Katie Lawrence, and Jack Shelton for proofreading, Marie Greenwood and Jolyon Goddard for editorial assistance, Emma Hobson for design assistance, Helen Peters for compiling the index, Dan Crisp for illustrations. The publishers would also like to thank Dr. Shannon Lucid for the "Meet the expert" interview.

The publisher would like to thank the following for their kind permission to reproduce their photographs:

(Key: a-above; b-below/bottom; c-centre; f-far; l-left; r-right; t-top)

2 **NASA:** (br); Jerry Woodfill (bl). 3 **Dorling Kindersley:** Andy Crawford (tr). **Dreamstime. com:** Yael Weiss (bc/Magnifying glass). **Getty Images:** QAI Publishing / UIG (cb). **NASA:** Bill Ingalls (br); Desiree Stover (bl); JSC / Stanford University (bc). 4-5 **ESA / Hubble:** NASA. 4 **ESO:** (crb). 5 **123RF.com:** qq47182080 (crb). **Dreamstime.com:** Mozzyb (clb); Levgenii Tryfonov / Trifff (tr). 6-7 **Dreamstime.com:** Andreykuzmin (Background). 6 **iStockphoto. com:** ZU_09 (bl); Wynnter (r). 7 **Getty Images:** Popperfoto (br); Time Life Pictures / Mansell / The LIFE Picture Collection (cl). 8-9 **123RF. com:** apostrophe. **ESO:** J. Emerson / VISTA. Acknowledgment: Cambridge Astronomical Survey Unit (Nebula). 8 **Alamy Stock Photo:** SPUTNIK (tr). **Getty Images:** Sovfoto / UIG (clb). **NASA:** (crb). 9 **Alamy Stock Photo:** SPUTNIK (tl). **NASA:** (cr); JSC (clb). 10 **NASA:** (cl, bl, tr). 10-11 **NASA:** (bc). 11 **NASA:** (tc, cl, br). 12 **ESA:** ATG medialab; background: ESO / S. Brunier (c). **NASA:** JPL-Caltech (bl). 13 **Getty Images:** Pallava Bagla / Corbis (bc); Sergei Fadeichev\TASS (tl); VCG (cra); The Asahi Shimbun (br). 14 **NASA:** (ca, clb). 14-15 **NASA:** (t). 15 **NASA:** (ca, b). 16-17 **Getty Images:** Mark Wilson. 16 **Getty Images:** Stan Honda / AFP (tc). **NASA:** (bc). **The National Archives of the UK:** National Archives photo no. 80-G-32500 (cla). 17 **NASA:** (bc). 18 **Getty Images:** Red Huber / Orlando Sentinel / TNS (l); VCG (r). 19 **Alamy Stock Photo:** Dinodia Photos (l). **NASA:** (tc); Bill Ingalls (r). 20 **Alamy Stock Photo:** Keystone Pictures USA / ZUMAPRESS (bl). 20-21 **Getty Images:** Scaled Composites (ca). **NASA:** (t); MSFC (cb). **Reaction Engines Limited:** (b). 22-23 **NASA.** 24-25 **NASA.** 25 **Dorling Kindersley:** Dave

Shayler / Astro Info Service Ltd (ca, ca/Apollo 8, c, c/Apollo 10, c/Apollo 12, cb, cb/Apollo 15, bc, bc/Apollo 17). 26 **NASA:** Bill Stafford (bl). 26-27 **NASA.** 27 **Alamy Stock Photo:** Andy Morton (cr). 28 **Avalon:** Liu Chan (cl). **Getty Images:** NASA (bc). 29 **NASA:** (bc). 30 **NASA:** (bc); Kim Shiflett (tr). 31 **NASA:** (br). 32 **ESA:** NASA (br). **Getty Images:** NASA / Roger Ressmeyer / Corbis / VCG (cb). **NASA:** (cl, cra). 33 **NASA:** (t, cl, r); Bill Ingalls (bl). 34 **NASA:** JPL (cb). 34-35 **NASA:** (ca). 35 **Alamy Stock Photo:** Keystone Pictures USA (tr); Xinhua (crb). **NASA:** (cb). 36-37 **NASA.** 37 **NASA:** (c, crb, bc). 38 **NASA:** (l). 39 **NASA:** Johns Hopkins University Applied Physics Laboratory / Southwest Research Institute (crb); JPL (t). 40 **123RF.com:** Pere Sanz (c). **Fotolia:** eevl (b/ Spiral galaxy). **NASA:** (tr, tr/Galaxy); Ames / JPL-Caltech / T Pyle (b). 41 **Dorling Kindersley:** Andy Crawford (cl/Telescope). **ESA / Hubble:** NASA (cl). **Fotolia:** dundanim (b/Earth). **NASA:** JPL (tr); Sonoma State University / Aurore Simonnet (b). 42-43 **NASA:** Pat Rawlings, (SAIC). Technical concepts for NASA's Exploration Office, Johnson Space Center (JSC). 43 **Foster + Partners:** (crb). **NASA:** (cra). 44 **Dorling Kindersley:** Stephen Oliver (ca). **Getty Images:** SSPL (crb). **NASA:** (bc, tr, c); Goddard (bl). 45 **Getty Images:** QAI Publishing / UIG (c). **NASA:** Johns Hopkins University Applied Physics Laboratory / Southwest Research Institute (clb); JPL (tc, bc); JPL-Caltech (cb). 46-47 **NASA:** (t). 46 **Getty Images:** Mark Greenberg / Virgin Galactic (cr). 47 **Blue Origin:** (c). 48 **Dorling Kindersley:** Liberty's Owl, Raptor and Reptile Centre, Hampshire, UK (cra). **Dreamstime.com:** Jahoo (ca). 48-49 **Science Photo Library:** Sputnik (ca). 49 **Depositphotos Inc:** Rukanoga (ca/ Tardigrade). **NASA:** JSC (ca). 50-51 **Dreamstime.com:** Geopappas (Paper clip). 50 **Dreamstime.com:** Yael Weiss (br/Magnifying glass). **NASA:** JPL-Caltech / SETI Institute (tr); Greg Shirah (clb); JPL-Caltech (crb); JSC /

Stanford University (br). 51 **Dreamstime.c** Dennis Van De Water (clb). **Getty Images:** Andrew Caballero-Reynolds / AFP (tc). 52 **Getty Images:** Sovfoto / UIG (c). **NASA:** Eugene Cernan (cb). 52-53 **Dreamstime.c** Amabrao (Border); Jason Winter / Eyematri (Tyre). 53 **Getty Images:** AFP (cra). **NASA:** JPL-Caltech / MSSS (clb); Jerry Woodfill (cla JPL-Caltech (crb). 54 **NASA:** (tl, cra). 55 **NA** Tony Landis (tr); (cla, c). 56-57 **NASA:** JPL-Caltech. 57 **NASA:** (tr, br); Desiree Stov (clb). 58-59 **ESA / Hubble:** NASA (t). 58 **ES Hubble:** NASA (br). 59 **Dreamstime.com:** Scol22 (tr). **NASA:** (tl, cr); Norman Kuring, NASA's Ocean Biology Processing Group. S by Kathryn Hansen and Pola Lem (cr/Black Bill Ingalls (bl). 60 **NASA:** (br). 64 **Dreamsti com:** Mozzyb (tl).

Endpaper images: *Front:* **Alamy Stock Photo:** Pictorial Press Ltd ftl; **NASA:** tc, ca, GSFC fcrb, JPL-Caltech bc (Cassini), fcr; *Back:* **Alamy Stock Photo:** SPUTNIK cla; **NASA:** bl, ca, bc, bc (Floating Free), cra, br.

Cover images: *Front:* **Dorling Kindersley** Dave Shayler / Astro Info Service Ltd cra; **NASA:** c; **Science Photo Library:** NASA cr *Back:* **Dreamstime.com:** Scol22 cla; **Scien Photo Library:** SPUTNIK cr; *Spine:* **Dreamstime.com:** Konstantin Shaklein / 3dsculptor cb; *Front Flap:* **Dorling Kindersley:** Bob Gathany cla/ (Lunar mod Dave Shayler / Astro Info Service Ltd cb; **NASA:** ca, ca/ (Atlantis), c, cr, br, tl/ (2), br/ Bill Ingalls clb/ (2), Johns Hopkins Universit Applied Physics Laboratory / Southwest Research Institute cla, Jerry Woodfill bc; *Ba Flap:* **NASA:** cb, Hubble Heritage Team, ES cb/ (Galaxy).

All other images © Dorling Kindersley
For further information see:
www.dkimages.com

My Findout facts:

Evolution of spacesuits

SK-1 pressure spacesuit, 1961

This spacesuit was worn by Yuri Gagarin when he became the first person in space, and by other cosmonauts on Vostok missions.

The suit had a mirror in the sleeve. This helped the cosmonaut locate switches that were hard to see.

Project Mercury spacesuit, 1961

The helmet could be removed once in orbit.

The spacesuit had 13 zippers, which ensured a good fit

America's first astronauts flew in the one-man Mercury spacecraft, and their spacesuit was a modified version of the Navy Mark IV pressure suit, used by fighter pilots.

Project Gemini spacesuit, 1965

The helmet included earphones and microphones

Extra layers were added for working outside the spacecraft

The spacesuit for the two-man Gemini missions was based on the high-altitude pressure suit worn by pilots of the X-15 rocket plane.

Apollo 11 spacesuit, 1969

This famous photo shows Buzz Aldrin wearing the A7L spacesuit. When worn on the Moon it included a Portable Life Support System "backpack".

Special lunar overshoes provided extra grip on the Moon's surface

BRAINSE DOMHNACH MIDE

DONAGHMEDE BRANCH

TEL: 8482833